Profit from Your Forecasting Software

Wiley & SAS Business Series

The Wiley & SAS Business Series presents books that help senior-level managers with their critical management decisions.

Titles in the Wiley & SAS Business Series include:

Analytics: The Agile Way by Phil Simon

Analytics in a Big Data World: The Essential Guide to Data Science and Its Applications by Bart Baesens

A Practical Guide to Analytics for Governments: Using Big Data for Good by Marie Lowman

Bank Fraud: Using Technology to Combat Losses by Revathi Subramanian

Big Data Analytics: Turning Big Data into Big Money by Frank Ohlhorst

Big Data, Big Innovation: Enabling Competitive Differentiation through Business Analytics by Evan Stubbs

Business Analytics for Customer Intelligence by Gert Laursen

Business Intelligence Applied: Implementing an Effective Information and Communications Technology Infrastructure by Michael Gendron

Business Intelligence and the Cloud: Strategic Implementation Guide by Michael S. Gendron

Business Transformation: A Roadmap for Maximizing Organizational Insights by Aiman Zeid

Connecting Organizational Silos: Taking Knowledge Flow Management to the Next Level with Social Media by Frank Leistner

Data-Driven Healthcare: How Analytics and BI Are Transforming the Industry by Laura Madsen

Delivering Business Analytics: Practical Guidelines for Best Practice by Evan Stubbs

Demand-Driven Forecasting: A Structured Approach to Forecasting, Second Edition by Charles Chase

For more information on any of the above titles, please visit www.wiley.com.

Profit from Your Forecasting Software

A Best Practice Guide for Sales Forecasters

Paul Goodwin

WILEY

For general information on our other products and services or for technical support, please contact our Customer Care Department within the United States at (800) 762–2974, outside the United States at (317) 572–3993, or fax (317) 572–4002.

Wiley publishes in a variety of print and electronic formats and by print-on-demand. Some material included with standard print versions of this book may not be included in e-books or in print-on-demand. If this book refers to media such as a CD or DVD that is not included in the version you purchased, you may download this material at http://booksupport.wiley.com. For more information about Wiley products, visit www.wiley.com.

Library of Congress Cataloging-in-Publication Data is Available:

ISBN 978-1-119-41457-5 (Hardcover)
ISBN 978-1-119-41598-5 (ePDF)
ISBN 978-1-119-41600-5 (ePub)

Cover Design: Wiley
Cover Image: © kraphix/iStockphoto

Printed in the United States of America

10 9 8 7 6 5 4 3 2 1

To my parents, Sidney and Norma Goodwin

Contents

Acknowledgments

A number of people have assisted me during the preparation of this book. The teams at SAS and Wiley have been helpful in speedily answering my queries and encouraging me to progress the book. In particular, I would like to thank Sheck Cho, Mike Gilliland, Lauree Shepard, Emily Paul, Banurekha Venkatesan, and Siân Roberts. Thanks are also due to Eric Stellwagen of Business Forecast Systems, Inc.

Much of the book reflects what I have learned from my fellow researchers and those with whom I have conducted consultancy work. These are too numerous to mention in their entirety, but they include Robert Fildes, George Wright, Richard Lawton, Dilek Önkal, Kostas Nikolopoulos, John Boylan, Aris Syntetos, Michael Lawrence, and Fotios Petropoulos. Nevertheless, any views expressed in the book are my own and any errors are my responsibility.

I must also thank Len Tashman who has allowed me, for the last 12 years, to write a regular Hot New Research column for *Foresight: The International Journal of Applied Forecasting*, which he edits. This has motivated me to keep abreast of the very latest research into applied forecasting, much of which is covered in the book.

Finally, I thank my wife, Chris, for her patience and encouragement during the many hours I have spent in my study absorbed in the fascinating and challenging topic of demand forecasting.

Prologue

I once heard of a woman who was working late on a Friday afternoon in her office when her boss appeared.

"We've just lost our sales forecaster," he said. "He's transferring to Customer Relations so we need someone to do his job from Monday. I'd like you to take on that role."

When the woman protested that she had no relevant experience in forecasting or any knowledge of statistics, the boss was reassuring.

"You'll soon pick it up. I think it's mostly done by the computer, anyway."

And with that he was gone.

If you find yourself in a similar position, then this is the book for you. Research indicates that many forecasters in companies, who may be experts in their products and markets, have little or no formal knowledge of forecasting methods. They are also not mathematicians, so explanations of these methods that befuddle them with reams of formulae and complex notation are of little help. This leads to a temptation to sidestep the methods. Allow the computer to produce its mysterious forecasts, but then replace them with finger-in-the-air judgments; or even avoid the computer altogether and fit a ruler roughly across a hand-drawn sales graph.

Even if you are willing to work with the computer, the technical terms it displays may seem forbidding. MSEs, MAPEs, AICs, exponential smoothing, *R*-squared, ARIMA models, and autocorrelations can sound as meaningful as the language of quantum physics is to the layperson. And yet, unlike quantum physics, all of these terms can be made understandable to a nonspecialist manager, at least at the intuitive level. In fact, many of them represent very simple concepts that are much easier to comprehend than a typical tax return.

It's a pity if forecasters aren't harnessing the full power of methods that are embodied in modern forecasting software because they don't understand the methods or their output. This book aims to remedy this situation by providing accessible explanations and guidance on when to use different methods and measures. It addresses key practical questions such as:

- When, if ever, should management judgment be used to adjust or override a computer's forecast?
- Should I choose my own forecasting method or let the expert system in the software choose it?
- How should I use the software to handle product hierarchies or to plan safety stock levels?
- How much past data should I use to fit and test my forecasting model?

The book is not tied to any specific forecasting software product. Nor is it intended to duplicate a user's manual, so it won't tell you which button to press or describe particular menu structures. Instead, it has an important complementary role. It draws on the very latest forecasting research to enable you to interact with your software with confidence and insight so you can aim for maximum forecast accuracy, while also making the best use of your time. Depending on what you need to know, you can either read the book in its entirety or use it as a reference guide when you need an explanation, or an evaluation, of a particular method or metric. The focus is on commercial demand forecasting software products, so the book does not consider facilities that may be available in free software, such as R, though much of the content will still be relevant to R users. Also, there is no coverage of specialist software that uses neural networks or conjoint analysis.

Sales forecasts can rarely be perfectly accurate – if they are, the forecaster was either very lucky or was told the exact quantity of orders that were in the pipeline. The true challenge of forecasting is to avoid *unnecessary* inaccuracy caused by systematic bias, inefficient use of available information, or the wrong choice of method or its application. This book should help you to meet that challenge by employing best practices, so you can ultimately profit from your forecasting software.

CHAPTER **1**

Profit from Accurate Forecasting

1.1 THE IMPORTANCE OF DEMAND FORECASTING

Forecasts of demand for products and services can be crucial to the operations of most companies. Inventory planning, logistics planning, production scheduling, cash flow planning, decisions on staffing levels, and purchasing decisions can all depend on forecasts. Making these forecasts perform as well as possible will lead to improved customer service levels and so foster customer goodwill and retention. It will also lower costs. There will be less need for expensive emergency production runs, and there should be a reduction in the waste associated with excessive stock levels and unsold products.

Figures for the cost reductions or increased profits that companies achieve through improved forecasting can be hard to come by – most organizations don't publish them. However, one forecasting software company (www.catchbull.com) estimates that avoidable forecast errors can add between 2% and 4% to costs of production. They quote the case of one $15 billion firm where executives estimated that "we can drive up to $200 m of avoidable costs out of the business." A survey carried out by a Triple Point Technology in 2013 indicated that reductions in inventory levels resulting from improved forecast accuracy meant that a company with a $1 billion turnover could expect savings of between $5 million and $10 million. However, the same survey found that 40% of respondents admitted that they were "not currently leveraging the advantages of statistical modeling in their demand planning operations." Of course, it's in the interests of software companies to advertise these huge benefits, but common sense suggests that better-performing forecasts will significantly benefit a company's bottom line.

1.2 WHEN IS A FORECAST NOT A FORECAST?

A forecast is an honest statement of what we expect to happen at a future data, based on the information available at the time when we make the forecast. It is not necessarily what we hope will happen, so it is not the same as a target. In fact, in some circumstances we may be doubtful that a target will be achieved – we simply created it to motivate people to try to get as close to it as possible. Nor is it the same as a plan.

A plan is what we intend to happen, assuming the future is under our control. As we shall see, ideally a forecast will acknowledge that we are uncertain about the future and provide a measure of that uncertainty.

It is also important to distinguish a forecast from a decision. A decision is what we choose to do in the light of a forecast. We may have a demand *forecast* for next week of 2,000 units, so we *decide* to hold 2,200 units in stock at the start of the week in case demand exceeds the forecast. The 2,200 units is not a forecast – it's a decision.

Sometimes people are tempted to look at the possible demand levels that may occur at a future period and decide which one will best suit their interests. For example, I might forecast a demand for next month of 3,500 units, knowing that it will please senior managers and gain me some kudos, even though I don't truly expect this demand level to be achieved. Although I might call this a forecast, in reality I'm making a decision.

1.3 WAYS OF PRESENTING FORECASTS

1.3.1 Forecasts as Probability Distributions

We can present forecasts in several different ways. A probability distribution indicates the possible levels of demand and their associated probabilities. Table 1.1 is an example. Figure 1.1 displays the distribution. It shows that relatively low levels of demand are more probable than very high demands, so the distribution is skewed. Forecasts in this form are useful because they show the risks of

Table 1.1 A Probability Distribution of Demand

Next Month's Demand (Units)	Probability (%)
20 to 29	5
30 to 39	30
40 to 49	41
50 to 59	10
60 to 69	8
70 to 79	5
80 to 89	1

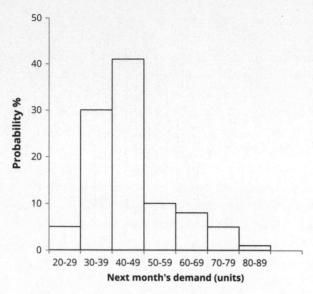

Figure 1.1 A graphical display of the probability distribution

particular decisions we may make. For example, if we decide to hold 69 units of stock at the start of the month, there will be a 5% + 1% = 6% probability that we will be unable to meet demand and will disappoint customers.

Accurately estimating probability distributions can be difficult, particularly if we have limited past data. Usually, it is assumed that a particular distribution applies and, most commonly, this is the bell-shaped normal or Gaussian distribution. Figure 1.2 shows an example. Notice that the distribution is symmetrical about its highest point. While there are theoretical reasons why a normal distribution will apply, in many circumstances it can at best only offer a rough approximation to the probabilities of future demand. When the "true" distribution is highly skewed, the approximation will be very poor.

1.3.2 Point Forecasts

Most software products don't currently display full probability distributions (sometimes these are called density forecasts). Instead, they produce point forecasts and prediction intervals. A point forecast is a

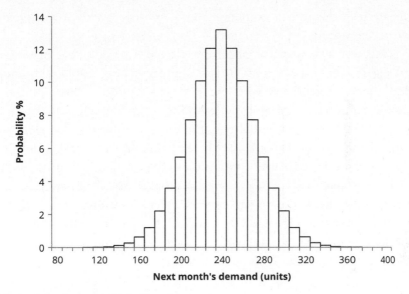

Figure 1.2 A normal distribution of demand

forecast expressed as a single number. It usually represents the mean (or average) of the probability distribution. Imagine if the month referred to in Figure 1.2 was repeated many times. On some occasions, we see demand greater than 300 units. On very rare occasions, it would exceed 350 units. In other months, demand might be well below 200 units. More often than not, it would be between 200 and 280. If we averaged all of the demands, we observed we would find that the mean demand was 240 units. This would be our point forecast. If we did the same for the month referred to in Figure 1.1, we would find that the mean demand was 45 units – slightly to the left of the range of possible demands because of the skewness in the distribution. Therefore, a point forecast produced by software is simply an average of all the possible levels of demand – taking into account their probabilities. It is not a statement that we think that that specific level of demand *will* occur – we know that the actual demand is likely to stray from its value as shown by the probability distributions. You might tell me the mean height of American males aged over 21, but I don't expect every American male I meet in this age group to be that height. In fact, meeting someone who conforms exactly to the mean would be rare.

This point is worth emphasising. I have heard of cases of senior managers who expect point forecasts always to be "100% accurate" and criticize forecasters who are not achieving this. Their attitude shows a fundamental misunderstanding of what a point forecast is. In most forecasting situations, there are bound to be random or unpredictable factors that cause the actual demand to stray from the average represented by the point forecast. In particularly unpredictable situations, such as when we forecast a long way ahead, we should not be surprised if the demand strays a significant distance from the point forecasts. However, as we will see, if we try to anticipate these random factors, we will be wasting our time and probably damaging the forecasts to boot.

1.3.3   Prediction Intervals

Point forecasts don't tell us anything about the level of uncertainty associated with a forecast. We can't tell how far actual demand might stray from the forecast, and you generally need this information to plan inventory levels. However, some idea of the level of uncertainty can be obtained from a prediction interval. A prediction interval is a range that has a stated probability of capturing the actual demand. For example, if we have the distribution shown in Figure 1.2, our software would produce a 95% prediction interval for next month's demand of 177 to 303 units. This means that there's a 95% chance that the actual demand will be captured within this range, and therefore, a 5% chance that the demand will be outside it.

The 95% is sometimes known as the coverage probability. Higher coverage probabilities and more uncertainty both lead to wider prediction intervals. Because of the greater uncertainty, prediction intervals therefore tend to be wider the further ahead you are forecasting. In Chapter 7, we will see how prediction intervals can be used to determine safety stocks and reorder levels. Note that sometimes prediction intervals are referred to as *confidence intervals*, though many statisticians prefer not to use that term in this context.

1.4 THE ADVANTAGES OF USING DEDICATED DEMAND FORECASTING SOFTWARE

Research into how companies make their sales forecasts indicates that spreadsheets are the most common of type of software employed. In one survey of US corporations, 48% of respondents used spreadsheets, while only 11% used specialized forecasting software. While spreadsheets may be accessible and allow plenty of flexibility, good-quality dedicated demand forecasting software offers many advantages.

First, they usually offer a wider range of forecasting methods than nondedicated software, and they automatically provide metrics allowing you to compare the accuracy of different methods (see Chapter 3). This increases the chances that you will find the most accurate forecasting method for a particular product. In addition, they are designed to support processes that are specific to demand forecasting such as bottom-up or top-down forecasting when you have a product hierarchy (see Chapter 7). Some software packages will also directly link your demand forecasts to inventory control, advising you on what your reorder level should be and how much safety stock you need to carry. Good-quality forecasting packages also have tried and tested algorithms to implement the different methods. It is known that statistical algorithms in some spreadsheet products contain errors that can result in serious inaccuracy in forecasting. Then there's the danger that you will introduce errors if you are setting up forecasting formulae in a spreadsheet yourself. Mistakes in cutting and pasting and references to the wrong cell ranges can compound the problem. One study found that companies who employed forecasting packages achieved average forecast errors that were almost 7% lower than those of spreadsheet users.

My experience when visiting some companies suggests that if people use a spreadsheet, there is also a danger they will set up an idiosyncratic forecasting system that no one else understands. If they leave the company, it's impossible for their successor to take over the system. Moreover, unlike methods available in good forecasting packages, these self-designed methods usually lack a theoretical underpinning, and they haven't been tested on lots of data sets or compared with other methods.

The second major reason for choosing dedicated software is that many aspects of the forecasting process can be automated and hence performed speedily. This can be particularly important in saving effort if you have to make a large number of forecasts on a frequent basis, and where timely forecasts are crucial to an organization's effectiveness. Even where fewer forecasts are needed, automation can take the form of automatic selection of a forecasting method, ideally with an associated explanation of why the method has been selected. Though automation may have some downsides (see Chapter 8), you will usually have the option of overruling the software's choice in cases where this seems necessary.

Finally, effective demand forecasting is often a team effort, involving forecasters, accounts managers, sales, and operations staff. Dedicated software is likely to be better at supporting collaboration than individuals' spreadsheets. In too many companies, there are *islands of analysis* – people producing their forecasts separately on non-interfacing, and sometimes homemade, systems. Often these systems have no direct connection with those used by production planners or other departments. Forecasters in a major retail company I visited had to copy data from one system using pen and paper, before manually reentering it into another system.

Some companies don't use computers at all to make their forecasts – they rely solely on the gut-feel of managers. As we'll see in Chapter 9, managers' judgments can bring benefits to forecasts if they are used where they are most appropriate. But we'll also see that, more often than not, judgmental forecasts suffer from both political and psychological biases that are inimical to accuracy. Replacing these with the forecasts from a dedicated forecast package is not only likely to reduce costs but also will allow managers to make more effective use of their time.

1.5 GETTING YOUR DATA READY FOR FORECASTING

Garbage in, garbage out has been a well-known phrase in computing for years and, of course, it applies to demand forecasting using computers as well. If you are supplying the software with erroneous data, then it will produce erroneous forecasts. Data cleansing is the process of removing errors and anomalies from the available data. It can be a time consuming and tedious task, but as we'll see, these days – with the availability of modern software – it should not be carried out too far. Moreover, if you use appropriate sources of data, it may be largely unnecessary.

First, we should note that our objective is to forecast future *demand* for a product or service, but historical data usually relates to *sales*. The two are not necessarily the same. Last month there may have been a demand for 2,500 units of your product, but because you only had 2,000 units available, you had sales of 2,000. In many situations, it's difficult to know how much demand was unfulfilled. Customers who saw an empty shelf where your product is usually displayed are unlikely to let you know that they were disappointed. However, some types of historical data are likely to be closer to demand than others.

Data on the quantities of a product shipped on particular dates may not reflect demand at that time because they might simply be delayed deliveries. Analysts agree that either point-of-sale (POS) or syndicated scanner data generally provide a better guide to demand. Syndicated scanner data can be obtained from specialist providers who use individually scanned purchases from large numbers of locations to build and then manipulate a database. This allows sales of products to be viewed at different levels of granularity – nationally, regionally, or at individual retail locations, or annually, quarterly, monthly weekly, or even daily. POS or syndicated scanner data is less likely to contain errors than data on past shipments that might have involved manual data entry, obviating the need to spend many joyless hours attempting to correct mistakes and chase down missing figures.

Even when historical data is correct, people can spend a lot of time cleansing it trying to remove unusual observations. These may be outliers such as exceptionally low sales figures caused by shortages of supplies or exceptionally high sales figures resulting from successful sales promotions. The worry is that these may distort forecasts, so attempts are often made to obtain *baseline* sales figures – that is, sales figures with the effects of shortages or promotions removed. The problem is that it's often difficult to know the size of the adjustment that should be applied to the anomalous sales figure. For example, how do you know how much of the sales uplift was due to a promotion and how much was simply caused by good weather that coincided with the promotion? When a promotion takes place at particular times of the year, how much of the spike in sales was simply a seasonal increase in demand that takes place every year at this time? The problem is particularly acute when, as is usual, judgment is being used to make the adjustment. As we'll see in Chapter 9, judgment can be subject to a range of cognitive biases.

The good news is that, when you have good-quality software, cleansing data for unusual events is likely to be generally unnecessary. You simply have to flag the observation as a special case, and the software will take care of the rest. In other cases, you may be using a model that employs data on demand drivers, such as advertising expenditure, to explain the sales patterns. This means that it can take into account unusual observations and even forecast when they will occur.

1.6 TRADING-DAY ADJUSTMENTS

One data preparation task that is usually well worth carrying out is adjusting past sales data for month lengths or the number of trading days. The demand for a product is likely to vary between months because they contain different numbers of days when the product is available for purchase. Weekends, national holidays, and the different lengths of months can all contribute to this variation and, if it is not taken into account, the software may falsely ascribe the variation to seasonality or randomness. Because we know the future calendar, this is an aspect of future demand that we can predict, so adjusting for the number of trading days tends to improve forecast accuracy.

Many forecasting software products will carry out the adjustments for you if you supply them with details of the relevant past and future numbers of trading days. If this facility is not available, one approach is to use the following steps:

1. Calculate the average number of trading days for the month in question (e.g., on average, how many trading days were there in October during the period for which you have data?). Call this A.

2. Determine the number of trading days for the specific month you are adjusting. Call this B.

3. Divide A by B to obtain the trading day weight.

4. Multiply the demand in the month in question by the trading day weight.

For example, suppose that the demand for a product in March of last year was 2,100 units and that month had 23 trading days. During our sales history, March on average had 22 trading days. Thus, $A = 22$ days and $B = 23$, so last March's trading day weight is $22/23 = 0.957$. This means its adjusted demand is $2,100 \times 0.957 = 2,010$ units. This puts last March's demand an equal footing with March's demand in other years. Because it had more than the average number of trading days, we have reduced its demand figure.

Once we have used the adjusted data to make the forecasts, we will need to readjust these to take into account the number of trading days in the future month. If we have a forecast of 3,000 units for March next year and it has only 20 trading days, then that March has a trading day weight of $22/20 = 1.1$. This time we *divide* the forecasted demand by the weight to give a revised forecast of $3000/1.1 = 2,727$ units.

This method assumes that all trading days are equally important. For example, if Tuesday is usually a busier trading day than Monday, then, ideally, we need to take into account the number of Mondays and Tuesdays in each month. Methods like regression analysis (see Chapter 6) can be used if this is the case.

1.7 OVERVIEW OF THE REST OF THE BOOK

Once your data is ready, you are all set to start making forecasts using your software. In the next chapter, we will look at how software searches for patterns in data so that it can project these ahead to produce forecasts. Chapter 3 looks at how the accuracy of forecasts can be measured and how biases, such as a systematic tendency to forecast too high, can be detected. The next three chapters explain how the most common methods for producing demand forecasts work and how to interpret the output from your software when you are using these methods.

Efficient inventory control is a key reason for demand forecasting, and Chapter 7 shows how you can use forecasts to determine when to place orders for new supplies and how to decide on safety stock levels. Often, we can arrange products into hierarchies to reflect their characteristics or markets. This chapter goes on to compare different methods for handling hierarchies that are available in some software products. It also discusses a method called *temporal aggregation* that can improve forecasts that guide inventory decisions.

Some software products will automatically suggest the best method for making forecasts in different situations and Chapter 8 explores when it is best to automate the forecasting process. It also considers whether complex forecasting methods are always more likely to give more accurate forecasts than simpler ones.

In contrast to automation, research shows that managers frequently use their judgment to override the forecasts generated by their software. Chapter 9 warns of the dangers of overzealous interventions and indicates when an override is likely to be justified.

Predicting the demand for new products is one of the most challenging tasks facing forecasters because of the lack of available historical demand data. However, historical data is often available for similar products launched in earlier periods. Chapter 10 shows how forecasting software can be used to exploit this data. It also looks at the potential pitfalls of using management judgment when forecasting the demand for new products.

The final chapter identifies the key attributes of a good-quality forecasting software product and provides a summary of the key messages in the book.

1.8 SUMMARY OF KEY TERMS

Sales and demand.   Demand is the amount of a product that could be sold if there were always sufficient supplies available to meet it. The amount actually sold will be less than demand when stock-outs have occurred, so some demand is unfulfilled.

Probability distribution.	A forecast that indicates the possible levels of demand together with the probability that each level will occur.
Normal or Gaussian distribution.	A probability distribution that is often used to approximate the true probability distribution of demand. It assumes that the chances of demand being above or below average are the same and that the probability of particular levels of demand declines the further they are from the average. When plotted as a histogram it resembles a bell shape.
Point forecast.	A forecast presented as a single number.
Prediction interval.	A range that has a specified probability of capturing the actual level of demand between its lower and upper limits.
Trading-day adjustments.	Changes made to historic sales data to take into account variations in the number of days a product was traded in different months.

1.9 REFERENCES

Chase, Jr., C. W. (2015). Cleanse your historical shipment data? Why? *Journal of Business Forecasting*, **34**, 29–33.

Field, P. J. (2006). On the use and abuse of Microsoft Excel. *Foresight*, **3**, 46–47.

Kamal, J. (2013). Best practice demand planning meets unprecedented demand volatility. *Supply and Demand Chain Executive* (December 5). http://www.sdcexec.com/article/11267412/research-shows-how-best-practice -demand-planning-contributes-to-the-challenge-of-accurate-forecasting -in-an-era-of-global-demand-uncertainty

McCullough. B. D. (2006). The unreliability of Excel's statistical procedures. *Foresight*, **3**, 44–45.

Moon, M. A., Mentzer, J. T., & Smith, C. D. (2003). Conducting a sales forecasting audit. *International Journal of Forecasting*, **19**(1), 5–25.

Sanders, N. R., and Marodt, K. B. (2003). Forecasting software in practice: use satisfaction and performance. *Interfaces*, **33**, 90–93.

CHAPTER **2**

How Your Software Finds Patterns in Past Demand Data

2.1 INTRODUCTION

The algorithms embodied in forecasting software are designed to identify and measure patterns in past data. The computer then makes forecasts assuming that these past patterns will continue into the future. Depending on the forecasting method used, the computer can search for two main types of patterns:

1. Patterns in the sales history – these may include features such as trends or seasonal patterns;
2. Relationships between sales and other factors – for example, sales may be related to the previous month's advertising expenditure or the product's current price.

In this chapter, we'll first look at the types of patterns that are commonly found in sales histories. Then we'll discuss how relationships between sales and the factors that might influence them can be revealed.

2.2 KEY FEATURES OF SALES HISTORIES

No matter how sophisticated the software you are using is, it's always a good idea to study a graph of your data to get a feel for what is going on. This can also enable you to carry out a sanity check on any results that the computer might produce. All good forecasting software products provide graphs of sales histories. Figure 2.1 is typical, depicting the quarterly sales of a product over five years. The pattern we see can be broken down into a three main components.

2.2.1 An Underlying Trend

Despite the short-term peaks and troughs in the graph, it can be seen that there is an underlying upward movement in sales. The period-to-period change in underlying sales level is the trend. In this case, we can estimate it roughly by putting a ruler through the graph (see the dotted line in Figure 2.1). This suggests that underlying sales levels have risen from about 40 to 120 units over 20 quarters – an increase of roughly 4 units each quarter. Hence, the trend is estimated to be about +4 units.

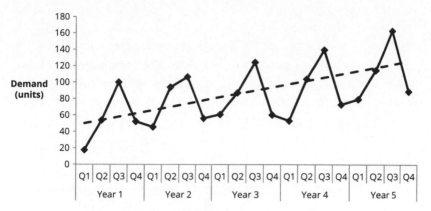

Figure 2.1   Demand history with trend and seasonal pattern

In Figure 2.1 the trend is linear – we could get a good estimate of it using the ruler. This indicates that each new quarter has seen the same increase in underlying sales over the previous quarter. Of course, there's no reason why trends have to be linear, or why they will stay the same forever. Indeed, underlying sales are unlikely to go on increasing at the same rate in the long term. As we approach market saturation, it will become increasingly difficult to find new customers, so the trend is likely to be damped, as shown in Figure 2.2a. A similar damping pattern is also often observed in downward trends – as sales approach zero, action may be taken to slow the decline and, in most situations, sales cannot go below zero, anyway.

Over time the trend is likely to change. Figure 2.2b shows a changing linear trend and, in Chapter 4, we'll show how the computer attempts to detect these changes. One reason for a changing trend in the long term is the economic cycle. The sales of many products will rise and fall as the economy moves from booms to slumps and consumers have less or more money spend. Another reason is the life cycle of a product as it evolves from its introduction through sales growth to maturity before it eventually declines in popularity (Figure 2.2c). Finally, Figure 2.2d shows an exponential trend.

2.2.2   A Seasonal Pattern

Overlaid on the trend in Figure 2.1 is a regular annual cycle in sales which peaks in quarter 3 (July to September) and has a trough in

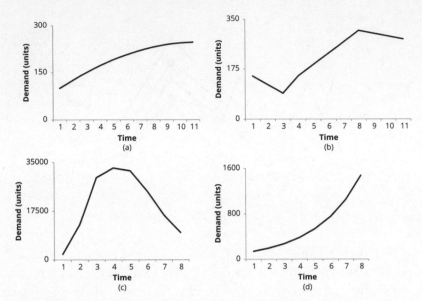

Figure 2.2 Examples of trend types: (a) Damped; (b) Changing linear; (c) Product life cycle; (d) Exponential

quarter 1 (January to March). This consistent seasonal cycle is clearly seen in the seasonal cycle graph in Figure 2.3, where each year's demand figures have been superimposed on each other.

The sales of a surprising number of products are subject to seasonal effects. Seasonal variations in the length of days, the weather, habits, traditions like Christmas, and institutional practices (like budget periods) can all lead to seasonal patterns. A seasonal effect is measured by determining the extent to which sales at a particular time of year are typically above or below the trend line. For example, to what extent are ice cream sales in the summer typically above the trend line, and to what extent are they typically below it in the winter? There are two main types of seasonal patterns.

Additive seasonality exists where, at a particular time of year, we would expect sales to be a certain number of units above or below the trend line – irrespective of the level of the underlying sales. For example, in Figure 2.1, sales are typically about 40 units above the trend line in quarter 3 in every year, irrespective of whether we are

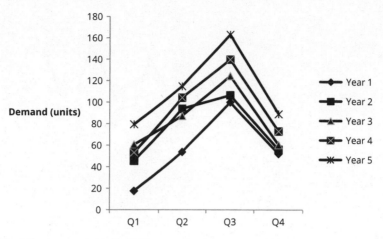

Figure 2.3 A seasonal-cycle graph

looking at an early year when underlying sales were relatively low or a later year when they were higher. Because sales in quarter 3 are typically 40 units above the trend line, we can say that quarter 3 has a seasonal index of +40. It can be shown that the seasonal indices for quarter 1, 2, and 4 are −30, +10, and −20 units, showing, for example, that quarter 1's sales are typically 30 units below the trend line. Figures 2.4a and 2.4b show other examples of additive seasonal patterns.

Seasonal patterns are sometimes more like those shown in Figures 2.5a and 2.5b. Here, the extent to which sales deviate from the trend line depends on the underlying level of sales. When the trend line is at a high level, the deviation is much greater than when it is at a lower level. This is multiplicative seasonality. We can no longer say that typically quarter 3 sales are certain number of units above the trend line as the deviation varies, depending on the underlying level of sales. But we can say that the deviation is typically a certain *multiple* of the underlying sales level. For example, in Figure 2.5a the quarter 3 sales are typically 1.8 times the underlying sales level, so this is the seasonal index for quarter 3. The indices for quarters 1, 2, and 4 are 0.6, 1.2, and 0.4, respectively, so, for example, quarter 4 sales are typically only 40% of the underlying sales level, and so well below it.

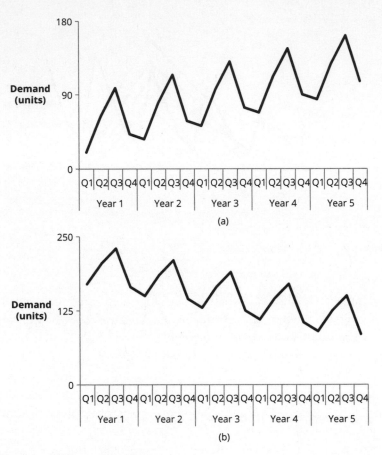

Figure 2.4 Additive seasonal patterns

Of course, there's no reason for seasonal patterns to stay constant over time. For example, changing fashions can lead to products becoming more popular in months when, in earlier years, they did not sell well, or vice versa. Also, movable festivals like Easter can mean that sales in different years can have different seasonal patterns. We will look at how forecasting software handles these issues later.

In some situations, repeated patterns, like those seen in seasonal cycles, can occur over shorter, or even longer, periods than a year. For example, the sales of some products may have a weekly pattern, with sales on a Monday always being relatively low, while those on a Saturday are relatively high. In these cases, we can apply the same methods

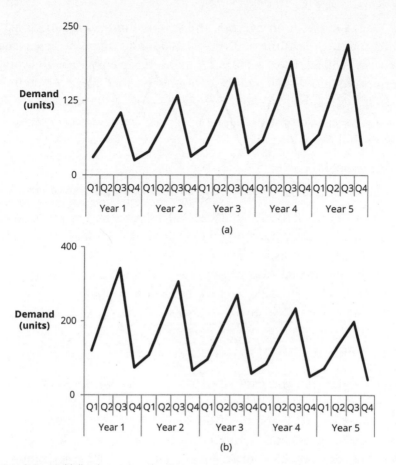

Figure 2.5 Multiplicative seasonal patterns

that are used to detect seasonal patterns; so, for example, Monday might have a "seasonal" index of 0.7 and Saturday, 1.6. Sometimes several of these repeated patterns are overlaid on each other. For example, sales of electricity usually have cycles that follow the time of day, the day of the week, and the week of the year.

Sometimes it is necessary to remove the seasonal element from a sales history before making forecasts. To deseasonalize sales that have an *additive seasonal pattern* you simply use the following formula:

Deseasonalized sales

= Actual sales – Average seasonal index for that time of year

For example, if on average, the seasonal index for June is +230 units and this year June had sales of 1000 units, then the deseasonalized sales will be: 1,000 − 230 = 770 units. If November has an average seasonal index of −300 and this November actual sales are 500 units, then the deseasonalized sales are: 500 − (−300) = 800 units.

To deseasonalize sales that have a *multiplicative seasonal pattern* you use the following formula:

Deseasonalized sales

= Actual sales/Average seasonal index for that time of year

For example, if the average seasonal index for March is 0.7 and this March has actual sales of 800 units, then the deseasonalized sales are: 800/0.7 = 1,143 units.

Note that the deseasonalized sales are not the same thing as the underlying level of sales, as they still contain random variation or noise. We discuss noise next.

2.2.3 Noise

Suppose that your company sells tires. One day, Mr. Jones drives over a nail and damages one of his car's front tires beyond repair. As a result, your sales go up by one tire. This small blip in sales could not have been predicted, and it falls into the third component of sales histories – noise, or the irregular component. When noise is a small component of sales, it gives the edge of the sales graph a jagged appearance. When it is more dominant, the graph looks more volatile, and it may be difficult to discern any regular patterns that are hidden beneath the noise.

Forecasting software is designed to extract these regular patterns by filtering out the noise. This means that when these patterns are extrapolated into the future to produce point forecasts, they are only estimates of what will happen if there is no noise. As we saw in the last chapter, essentially they represent an estimate of what would happen *on average* in a future period if that future period could be repeated many times over. Because of noise, the actual sales will vary around this average so that the forecast will seldom be the same as the sales that occur. Ironically, this means that you can never say that an individual computer-based forecast is wrong. It's a forecast of an average and you never see the average, only an individual sales value.

However, it's still important to measure how much variation in sales is caused by noise. This will give us an idea of the extent to which the actual sales are likely to stray from our point forecast. We will need this guidance when deciding on how much safety stock to carry to meet unexpectedly high demand for a product. Note that in many sales series, the noise tends to be greater the higher the levels of sales. Forecasting methods that acknowledge this are called proportional error methods (or models).

2.3 AUTOCORRELATION

Another feature of sales histories can be useful in forecasting, particularly where a casual inspection of the graph suggests there is no systematic pattern that can be extrapolated. This is called *autocorrelation* (literally "correlation with itself"). As we'll see later, correlation is a measure of the extent to which two things are associated. For example, high advertising expenditure may be associated with high sales and low expenditure with low sales. In contrast, autocorrelation is a measure of the extent to which sales values are correlated with other sales values that occurred earlier. For example, higher than average sales in each week may be associated with higher than average sales in the following week, and vice versa. Because high sales in each week are associated with high sales in the subsequent week, this is an example of a positive autocorrelation. In other circumstances, higher than average sales in each week may be associated with lower than average sales in the week that follows, perhaps because, in weeks when people stocked up early, they had less need to buy the product in their next weekly shop. This would be an example of negative autocorrelation. Autocorrelation does not just apply to consecutive periods. In some circumstances, we may find that sales several periods apart are associated. For example, sales seven days apart are typically positively autocorrelated for obvious reasons.

Autocorrelation is measured on a scale from −1, perfect negative autocorrelation to +1, perfect positive autocorrelation. In practical forecasting, these values are rarely encountered – they imply that you could make a perfectly accurate forecast if you know the value of the relevant earlier sales value. The closer the autocorrelation is to either −1 or +1, the stronger is the association. A value of zero indicates that no autocorrelation has been detected. Values close to zero mean the autocorrelation is weak, and it may be that the true value is zero and chance patterns in the noise have led to an error in its estimation.

The weekly sales in Figure 2.6a don't seem to follow an obvious pattern. However, Figure 2.6b, known as a plot of an autocorrelation function, shows that sales one week apart (i.e., with a lag of one week) have an autocorrelation of +0.47. Further analysis would reveal that this is unlikely to have arisen by chance. It appears that if we had higher than average sales this week, we can expect higher

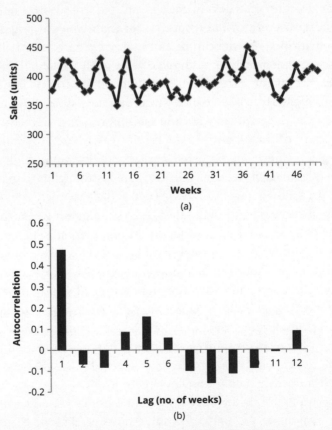

(a)

(b)

Figure 2.6 Plot of sales history and associated autocorrelation function

than average sales next week, though, of course, the actuals sales will also be affected by noise. Similarly, lower than average sales in one week will tend to be followed by lower than average sales in the following week. The autocorrelations between sales that are two weeks apart or more are much smaller and are probably simply reflecting chance patterns. Care needs to be taken when using autocorrelation in forecasting. The Box-Jenkins forecasting method that we will meet in Chapter 5 provides a structured approach to testing for autocorrelations and exploiting these to generate forecasts.

2.4 INTERMITTENT DEMAND

In some cases, such as the sales of spare parts, the demand pattern can look like the one in Table 2.1.

Here, weeks when there is demand for the product are interspersed with periods of zero demand. In addition, when there is demand for the product, there can be considerable variation in its size. Intermittent demand poses particular challenges to demand forecasters, but a number of methods are available in software products that are designed to cope with it. These include Croston's method, which we will meet in Chapter 4.

2.5 OUTLIERS AND SPECIAL EVENTS

Sales histories sometimes contain unusually low or high values, or *outliers*. These may result from planned events, such as sales promotions, or freak circumstances, such as exceptional weather conditions. Sometimes they occur because of errors made when someone enters data into the computer – for example, recording sales of 100 units as 1,000. Outliers can pose problems for some forecasting methods because they can distort estimates of features such as trends, seasonal patterns and autocorrelation. Because of this, many software products

Table 2.1 Intermittent Demand

Week	1	2	3	4	5	6	7	8	9	10
Demand (units)	14	5	0	0	95	10	0	16	0	0

have facilities for detecting outliers. Usually, the sensitivity of the detection method can be adjusted to suit the user. If he or she desires, outliers can then be corrected by replacing them with values that are more typical before producing the forecasts.

The decision on whether to correct outliers is a judgment call. Correcting the occasional extreme outlier will probably improve your forecasts. But if the process is carried out with excessive zeal, so that even moderate outliers are corrected, then the forecasting process is likely to underestimate the amount of randomness associated with the forecasts. This may lead to underestimation of the potential for the actual demand to stray from the forecasts leading to insufficient safety stocks being held.

An alternative way of dealing with exceptional conditions is to use an event index. This involves indicating to the software when a special event has occurred. The software then estimates the effect of this event on sales. The result is similar to a seasonal index and, like a seasonal index, it can be additive (e.g., the effect of the event was to increase sales, so they were 240 units above the underlying sales level) or multiplicative (e.g., the effect of the event was to increase sales, so they were 1.3 times the underlying sales level). This approach means that that the exceptional sales will have no effect on forecasts for periods that are considered to be normal.

However, sometimes special events are repeated. For example, having had a sales promotion five months ago, you may be planning another promotion for next month. If you tell the software that the special event will occur again next month, it will use the event index it previously estimated to modify next month's forecast, so the effect of the promotion is automatically built into the forecast. Another advantage of event indexes is that you can distinguish between different special events. For example, you may want to distinguish between promotions involving price discounts and those providing free gifts, or those offering prizes in competitions. The software will make separate estimates of the effects of these different types of events. Event indexes can also be used to handle repeated events that occur in different weeks, depending on the year, such as Easter, Ramadan, and Independence Day in the United States. You simply indicate when these events occurred in the past and when they are due to occur. The software will do the rest.

In many companies, managers prefer to use their judgment to adjust forecasts for special events. However, as we'll see in Chapter 9, research suggests that these adjustments are often biased, and there's some evidence that letting the software make the adjustments through event indices is likely to lead to more accurate forecasts.

2.6 CORRELATION

Rather than looking for patterns in sales histories, we can sometimes get more accurate forecasts by identifying the factors that are driving sales. For example, sales of our product may be influenced by the number of pages of newspaper advertising that we buy or the price that we are charging. Figure 2.7 is a scattergraph showing the national sales of a product in each of 40 weeks plotted against the number of supermarkets nationwide who are offering a price discount on the product. We can make three observations about the scatter of points on the graph. First, the association is positive – when more supermarkets offer the discount, we tend to see higher sales. Second, the association is strong, but not perfect. If we know how many supermarkets are offering the discount, we still cannot predict sales with perfect accuracy. Third, we can summarize the underlying association with a straight line – just like the ruler we used earlier – so it appears to be linear.

Correlation is a measure of the direction and strength of association between two variables and is usually represented by the letter r or R. Like autocorrelation, it is measured on a scale from -1 to $+1$. In Figure 2.7, the value of r is $+0.84$. Figure 2.8 shows some other examples of associations and their respective r values. In Figure 2.8a, there is a strong negative association: Higher prices tend to be associated with lower sales. Figure 2.8b suggests that there is no association between the sales of two very different products.

It's important to note that r is only a measure of the strength of *linear* association. In Figure 2.8c, there is clearly a strong relationship between sales revenue and the unit price of a product – both a low price and a high price are detrimental to revenue as, in the latter case, it deters potential purchasers. However, the computer has given a value of almost zero for r, wrongly suggesting that there is no association, and that knowing the unit price would be of no use in forecasting sales revenue.

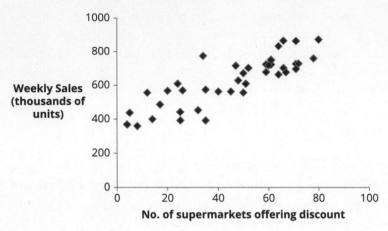

Figure 2.7 A scattergraph

Figure 2.8d shows the undue influence that an outlying value can have on the measurement of r. If the outlying value is removed, r is only −0.07. It's possible that the outlier simply resulted from a mistake in entering data.

These examples show the importance of studying a graph before drawing conclusions when the computer produces a value for r. Also, when you only have a few points on your graph, you should be careful before concluding that two variables are correlated. A small number of points might just happen to fall close to a linear pattern on the graph by pure chance, even when there is no real association between them. In Chapter 6, we'll look at how to assess whether apparent linear patterns have arisen by chance.

Finally, it's important to note that correlation does not prove that there is a causal link between the factor you are looking at and sales. Two variables can be correlated because they are both associated with a "hidden" third variable. For example, there is likely to be a strong correlation between deaths by drowning and ice cream sales, but it would be nonsensical to infer a causal relationship. Both factors are related to the weather.

In other cases, unrelated variables just happen to have increased over the same time period so that they turn out to be correlated. The population of Britain increased from 1984 to 2010, as did the percentage of American households with a computer. But it's unlikely that the

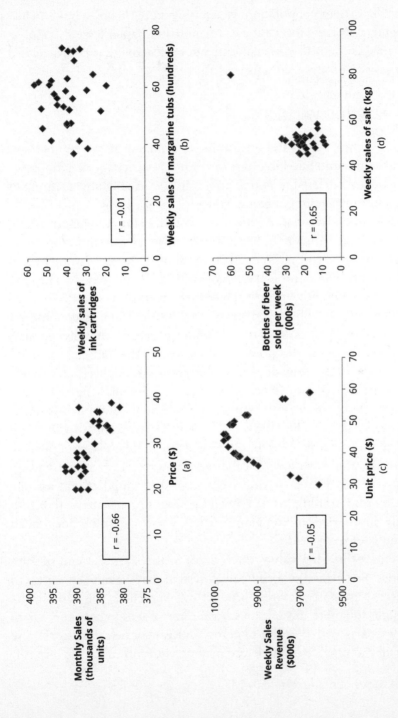

Figure 2.8 Examples of scattergraphs and correlations

29

growth in Britain's population was causing more US households to buy computers. Bearing these caveats in mind, in Chapter 6 we will look at how forecasting software enables us to use factors that are correlated with sales to produce sales forecasts.

2.7 MISSING VALUES

Often, we find that values are missing from our data sets, perhaps because someone has forgotten to record a particular sales figure or has accidently deleted it. Forecasting software usually offers a number of options for handling missing values.

One option is to remove any cases with missing data before asking the computer to analyze it. For example, if we have 40 months of data on sales and advertising expenditure, but one of the advertising figures is missing, the computer will work out the correlation based on just the 39 months when both variables have been recorded.

Alternatively, when you have sales history data, depending on your software, you can ask the computer to replace the missing sales figure with a zero, the previous sales figure, the subsequent sales, the average of the previous and subsequent sales figures, and so on. In the last case, if you have a gap of several periods where data are missing, the computer can estimate replacement values by assuming they would lie on a line drawn between the last recorded value and the one that follows the gap. Care needs to be taken when replacing a missing value with a zero; otherwise, your forecasts might end up being seriously biased. If you use a zero, the computer will assume that you sold nothing in the relevant period, so replacing with a zero is only appropriate in companies where a missing value does mean that no sales were made.

Series of missing values often occur at the start and end of sales histories. For example, a company's system may have been set up to start recording sales before a product was launched. You can ask the computer to ignore these values. Again, care needs to be taken where a series starts with a string of zeros, and it may be safest to ask the computer to remove them before making your forecasts.

2.8 WRAP-UP

1. Statistical forecasting methods attempt to filter out noise from historic sales data to detect underlying patterns. They then make forecasts based on the assumption that these patterns will continue into the future.

2. Sales histories often have trends and seasonal patterns. Trends can be linear or nonlinear and seasonal patterns can be additive or multiplicative.

3. Autocorrelation measures the extent to which sales are associated with sales that occurred a given number of periods earlier. It often reveals patterns in sales histories that appear to be random.

4. Historic patterns can also take the form of associations between sales and other variables like advertising expenditure and price. Correlation can be useful in detecting and measuring these associations, but it only measures associations that are linear and does not provide proof of a causal link between the variables.

5. It is wise to examine graphs of your data. Measures produced by the computer can be misleading if associations are not linear, or if the data contains outliers.

2.9 SUMMARY OF KEY TERMS

Underlying sales level.	The level of sales that remains in a period after we have removed estimates of seasonal effects, noise, and the effect of special events from the original sales figure.
Trend.	The difference between two consecutive underlying sales levels.
Linear trend.	A trend where the difference between consecutive underlying sales levels remains the same as history advances.

Additive seasonal pattern.	A seasonal pattern where actual sales can be expected to be a given distance from the underlying sales level at a particular time of year, irrespective of what that underlying sales level is. The expected distance is measured by a seasonal index.
Multiplicative seasonal pattern.	A seasonal pattern where the actual sales can be expected to be a given multiple of the underlying sales level (e.g., 0.4 times, or 1.6 times) at a particular time of year. In this case, the expected multiple is also measured by a seasonal index.
Noise.	The random movements in sales that cannot be accurately predicted.
Autocorrelation.	A measure of the strength of association between sales a given number of periods apart. In positive autocorrelation, higher than average sales in one period are associated with higher than average sales in a later period, while lower than average sales are associated with lower than average sales in the later period. In negative autocorrelation, higher than average sales in one period are associated with lower than average sales in the later period, and vice versa.
Event index.	The estimated extent to which actual sales depart from the underlying sales level because of a special event.
Correlation.	A measure of the strength and direction of the linear association between two variables. When correlation is positive, the two variables tend to increase and decrease together. When it is negative, as one variable increases, the other tends to decrease.

CHAPTER **3**

Understanding Your Software's Bias and Accuracy Measures

3.1 INTRODUCTION

Before we look at how forecasting software packages turn data into forecasts, we need to look at how to interpret bias and accuracy measures that are usually reported by software. *Bias* in forecasts usually refers to a persistent tendency for the forecasts to be too high or too low (though there are other types of bias). Detecting bias can be particularly important in learning how forecasts might be improved. One research study, by Nada Sanders and Gregory Graman in 2009, suggested that high levels of bias in forecasts can add considerably to a company's costs.

As we'll see, accuracy measures come in a variety of forms. They can represent the typical closeness of the forecast to the actual sales, measured in actual sales units or as percentages, or they can provide comparisons of the accuracy of a chosen forecasting method with a benchmark method. It's important to remember that there is almost certain to be a difference between a forecast and actual sales because of noise. A difference does not necessarily imply that the forecasting method has failed in some way. As we saw earlier, forecasting methods are not intended to anticipate noise. Some sales histories consist largely of noise, so large differences are to be expected since the product's sales are largely unpredictable. We should only consider changing a forecasting method after monitoring its performance over several periods and comparing this with the performance of alternative methods.

3.2 FITTING AND FORECASTING

When measuring the accuracy of a forecasting method, it's important to distinguish between the "fit" of the method and its "true" forecasting accuracy. When you supply historical sales data to your forecasting software, it will use this to identify the method and model that provides the most accurate fit to the historical underlying pattern. For each period in the history, the method will estimate a fitted sales value that is its estimate of the level of sales at that time once the effect of noise has been removed. The difference between the actual sales and the fitted value is called a residual.

The software will then report some of the measures that we will see in the following sections to tell you how good this fit was. However, although these measures are useful, they are likely to exaggerate the accuracy of the method when it comes to producing forecasts. That's because, when it determines which method to use, the computer has "seen" all the sales figures. To truly test a forecasting method, we should hide some of our sales data from it and see how well it forecasts sales that it hasn't seen.

To test a method, sales histories are therefore divided into fitting (or in-sample) periods, which enable the computer to decide what it thinks is the best method and model and hold-out (or out-of-sample) periods that allow us to see how well the chosen model forecasts sales it hasn't seen. Figure 3.1 shows a typical split.

When choosing between different forecasting methods, accuracy in forecasting sales in the hold-out sample is clearly the better guide. As we'll see later, it's always possible to find a forecasting model that perfectly fits sales in the in-sample periods. But when such a model is tested on the hold-out sample, it is likely to perform badly. This is because it will also be modeling the peculiarities of the noise that occurred in the in-sample periods, and these patterns are unlikely to reoccur in the future. Using a hold-out sample thus helps to guard against what is referred to as *overfitting*.

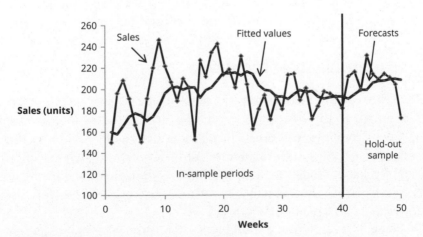

Figure 3.1 Fitting (in-sample) and hold-out periods

3.2.1 Fixed-Origin Evaluations

There are two ways we can use hold-out samples to evaluate a fore-casting method. The first way is to leave the end of the in-sample periods fixed at a certain point. In Figure 3.1 this would be week 40. The computer would then use the first 40 weeks to choose and esti-mate the forecasting model. We would then see how accurately the chosen method forecasts one period ahead to week 41, two periods ahead to week 42, and so on, ending with a 10-period-ahead forecast to week 50. All our forecasts originate from the information we have up to week 40. This is therefore called a fixed-origin evaluation.

A fixed-origin evaluation has three limitations. First, we will only have one forecast for each lead time. If our main interest is in fore-casting two weeks ahead, we will only have a single two-week-ahead forecast with which to judge the accuracy of the method with this lead time. Second, some forecasting software products would report the average accuracy of our 10 out-of-sample forecasts. But the 10-period-ahead forecast is likely to be far less accurate than the one- or two-period-ahead forecasts. Thus, the average accuracy reported would be based on a mixture of forecasts with different lead times, so it might not be typical of the accuracy we might expect at any specific lead time. Third, if, by bad luck, there happened to be something unusual about the sales in week 40 (e.g., they were unusually high), then this might distort the subsequent forecasts and give us a misleading impression of their typical accuracy.

3.2.2 Rolling-Origin Evaluations

We can partly address these three problems by using a rolling-origin evaluation. In this case, having recorded the accuracy of forecasts for weeks 41 to 50, as in Figure 3.1, the computer would then move the origin to week 41 and make forecasts from that origin for the remaining nine weeks. It would then repeat the process, incrementing the origin by one week at a time, until it only had to make one forecast – a forecast for week 50, from an origin of week 49.

Table 3.1 shows the number of forecasts we would get for the different lead times. It can be seen that we would have 10

Table 3.1 Rolling-origin Forecast Evaluation

Origin	Forecast for:									
	Week 41	Week 42	Week 43	Week 44	Week 45	Week 46	Week 47	Week 48	Week 49	Week 50
Week 40	1 pa	2 pa	3 pa	4 pa	5 pa	6 pa	7 pa	8 pa	9 pa	10 pa
Week 41		1 pa	2 pa	3 pa	4 pa	5 pa	6 pa	7 pa	8 pa	9 pa
Week 42			1 pa	2 pa	3 pa	4 pa	5 pa	6 pa	7 pa	8 pa
Week 43				1 pa	2 pa	3 pa	4 pa	5 pa	6 pa	7 pa
Week 44					1 pa	2 pa	3 pa	4 pa	5 pa	6 pa
Week 45						1 pa	2 pa	3 pa	4 pa	5 pa
Week 46							1 pa	2 pa	3 pa	4 pa
Week 47								1 pa	2 pa	3 pa
Week 48									1 pa	2 pa
Week 49										1 pa

pa = periods ahead

one-period-ahead forecasts. The computer would report the average accuracy of these 10 forecasts. It would also do this for the nine two-period-ahead forecasts, and so on. This would allow us to assess how accurate the forecasting method is likely to be for different lead times. Of course, we would only have a single 10-period-ahead forecast, so the estimate of the likely accuracy of forecasts for this lead time would have to be treated with caution. In some software products, the reports of accuracy in the form of Table 3.1 are referred to as waterfall reports. Note that not all software products reestimate the model when each extra observation becomes available as the origin moves forward.

How should you divide your sales history into in-sample and hold-out sample periods? If you have too few in-sample periods, then the computer will have insufficient information to estimate a reliable forecasting model. But if you have too few hold-out periods, then your estimates of the likely accuracy of the forecasting method will be unreliable.

In practice, the decision on this split is a judgment call, but there are some guidelines. First, the number of out-of-sample periods needs to be at least equal to how far ahead you are forecasting. If you are forecasting, say, six periods ahead, then you need at least six hold-out periods. However, if you stick to this minimum, then you will only have a single six-period-ahead forecast with which to evaluate your method. Increase your hold-out sample to seven periods and, if you are using a rolling origin, you'll now have two six-period-ahead forecasts to evaluate. This leads to the following procedure:

1. Determine your forecast lead time. Call this L.
2. Decide how many forecasts you need to assess accuracy. Call this A.
3. You will need $L + A - 1$ out-of-sample periods.

For example, suppose you are forecasting 12 months ahead and think that you need six forecasts at this lead time to get a reliable indication of a method's accuracy. In this case, $L = 12$ and $A = 6$ so you will need $12 + 6 - 1 = 17$ out-of-sample periods.

Of course, if we only have historical data on sales in, say, 25 months, then this would be problematical because we would only have eight in-sample periods to estimate our model. It would probably be better to reduce A, perhaps to 4. However, we would now have a smaller sample of "true" forecasts, so we should be cautious about reaching conclusions about our method's accuracy. It would be a good idea to monitor this over the next few months as new sales figures arrive.

We'll next look at how to measure the accuracy and bias of forecasts. All of the measures that we discuss can be used to measure both in-sample fit and out-of-sample accuracy. However, in the case of the relative accuracy measures, as we'll see, there is a slight difference in the procedure used depending on whether we are measuring fit or forecast accuracy. Of course, you won't need to calculate these measures yourself – the computer will do this for you. Nevertheless, it's useful to understand how they are worked out in order to see their advantages and disadvantages. These are summarized later in the chapter in Table 3.6.

3.3 FORECAST ERRORS AND BIAS MEASURES

Table 3.2 shows the sales of a product over 15 weeks and the forecasts made for these weeks one week earlier by a forecasting software product. The fourth column shows how close the forecasts were to

Table 3.2 Sales and Forecasts for a Product

No. of Units Sold	Forecasts	Error	Percentage Error
112	85	27	24.1
109	88	21	19.3
119	90	29	24.4
138	93	45	32.6
81	98	−17	−21.0
128	96	32	25.0
101	99	2	2.0
115	99	16	13.9
85	101	−16	−18.8
113	99	14	12.4
65	100	−35	−53.8
68	97	−29	−42.6
85	94	−9	−10.6
122	93	29	23.8
139	96	43	30.9
	Mean	10.1	4.1

the actual sales by displaying the forecast errors. The error is defined as Actual sales − Forecast (not the other way round), so the error for week one was $112 - 85 = 27$ units.

This means that a positive error indicates that the forecast was too low while a negative error indicates it was too high, which might seem to be counterintuitive. This will make more sense later when we see that adaptive forecasting methods use the errors, measured in this way, to try to adjust to new circumstances.

3.3.1 The Mean Error (ME)

The mean error (ME) is a measure of bias. In our case, the mean error over the 15 weeks is calculated by simply summing the errors and dividing by the number of forecasts. This gives $152/15 = 10.1$ units. Because this is positive, it suggests that there is a tendency to *under*forecast sales. If a method is unbiased, we would expect that, in the long run, the positive errors will cancel out the negative errors;

so, ideally, the mean error will be zero. Over a shorter period, like 15 weeks, it's unlikely that the mean error will be exactly zero. We should only be concerned if it is large relative to the actual sales. Even then, we should check that an isolated freak sales figure, an outlier, has not distorted the measure.

3.3.2 The Mean Percentage Error (MPE)

Table 3.2 also shows the errors as percentages of the actual values. For example, for week 1 the percentage error is $100 \times 27/112 = 24.1\%$. A percentage error is useful when we want an assessment of the seriousness of an error. For example, an error of 20 units would be trivial if we are forecasting sales of cans of baked beans, which sell in millions of units, but potentially disastrous if we are forecasting sales of passenger jets.

The mean percentage error (MPE) for the forecasts in Table 3.2 is found by simply summing the percentage errors to get 61.4% and dividing by 15 to obtain 4.1%.

We need to be careful when using measures based on percentage errors if we occasionally get very low, or even zero, sales. For example, if we make a forecast of sales of 6 units and the actual sales are 2 units, then we have an error of only −4 units. However the percentage error is $100 \times -4/2 = -200\%$. This would distort a measure like the MPE if all of the other percentage errors were relatively low. If some of our sales figures are zero, then the percentage error cannot be calculated, so the MPE is an unsuitable measure for products that have intermittent demand.

3.4 DIRECT ACCURACY MEASURES

3.4.1 The Mean Absolute Error (MAE)

The mean error cannot measure the accuracy of forecasts. For example, if in two consecutive weeks, we have errors of +2,000 units followed by −2,000 units, then the mean error is zero. This would suggest, wrongly, that our two forecasts have been perfectly accurate.

One way of assessing accuracy is to ignore the signs of the errors and to take the average of these absolute errors. The result is called

Table 3.3 Absolute and Squared Forecast Errors

No. of Units Sold	Forecasts	Absolute Errors	Squared Errors
112	85	27	729
109	88	21	441
119	90	29	841
138	93	45	2025
81	98	17	289
128	96	32	1024
101	99	2	4
115	99	16	256
85	101	16	256
113	99	14	196
65	100	35	1225
68	97	29	841
85	94	9	81
122	93	29	841
139	96	43	1849
		24.3	726.5
		MAE	MSE

the mean absolute error (MAE). Note that in some software products it is referred to as the mean absolute deviation (MAD). Table 3.3 shows the absolute errors for our example. The MAE is simply the sum of the absolute errors divided by the number of forecasts. This gives 364/15 = 24.3 units, so typically the forecasts were about 24 units off.

3.4.2 The Mean Squared Error (MSE)

Rather than ignoring the signs of the errors, to stop the negative and positive errors from canceling each other out, we can square them. The squared errors are displayed in Table 3.3. The mean squared error (MSE) is calculated by summing the squared errors and dividing by the number of forecasts. In our case, this gives 10898/15 = 726.5 squared units.

Note that, superficially, the MSE can make the accuracy of the forecasts look awful, and the concept of a squared sales unit is rather difficult to interpret. Because of this, some people prefer to take the square root of the MSE. This gives the root mean squared error (RMSE), which in our case is the square root of $726.5 = 27.0$ units.

Which is the best measure of accuracy, the MAE or the MSE? The MAE is easier to interpret, but ignoring the signs of the errors can make the method harder to analyze mathematically than the MSE. For example, the MSE can be broken down mathematically into components so that inaccuracies resulting from bias can be separated out. This leads to a measure called the unbiased mean squared error, which shows how accurate the forecasts would have been if we could have removed the bias. Some software products supply this measure, if requested.

By squaring the errors, the MSE penalizes large errors disproportionately. For example, after it's been squared, an error of 6 units is four times an error of 3 units. If you particularly want to avoid the occasional large error, the MSE can therefore be a useful guide when comparing alternative forecasting methods.

3.5 PERCENTAGE ACCURACY MEASURES

Is a mean absolute error of 25 units good or bad? As we saw earlier, this depends on the context. If sales are typically in thousands, it's probably an excellent level of accuracy. If they usually hover around the 50-unit mark, then we may have cause for concern. Percentage accuracy measures are designed to reflect the seriousness of errors by expressing the typical error as a percentage of actual or typical sales.

Percentage accuracy measures also have the advantage that they do not depend on the volume of your sales – for example, whether your sales are typically measured in tens, hundreds, thousands, or even millions of units. They are therefore said to be scale free. This means that you can compare the forecast accuracy of a method across different products whose sales volumes may vary considerably.

3.5.1 The Mean Absolute Percentage Error (MAPE)

To obtain the mean absolute percentage error (MAPE), the computer will calculate each error as a percentage of the actual sales (as with the MPE). However, any negative signs are then removed to obtain

Table 3.4 Absolute Percentage Errors

Week	No. of Units Sold	Forecasts	Absolute Errors	Absolute % Errors	Symmetric Absolute % Errors
1	112	85	27	24.1	27.4
2	109	88	21	19.3	21.3
3	119	90	29	24.4	27.8
4	138	93	45	32.6	39.0
5	81	98	17	21.0	19.0
6	128	96	32	25.0	28.6
7	101	99	2	2.0	2.0
8	115	99	16	13.9	15.0
9	85	101	16	18.8	17.2
10	113	99	14	12.4	13.2
11	65	100	35	53.8	42.4
12	68	97	29	42.6	35.2
13	85	94	9	10.6	10.1
14	122	93	29	23.8	27.0
15	139	96	43	30.9	36.6
Mean	105.3			23.7	24.1
				MAPE	SMAPE
				23.8	
				MDAPE	

the absolute percentage errors. The MAPE is simply the mean of these absolute percentage errors. The absolute percentage errors for our example are shown in Table 3.4. These are summed and divided by 15, the number of forecasts. This gives a MAPE of 23.7%. There has been some debate as to whether the absolute forecast error should be divided by the forecast, rather than the actual sales, when calculating the MAPE. There are advantages to both options, but most software products use the actual sales in the denominator.

Although the MAPE is widely used, as with the MPE, care should be taken when some sales figures are small. If an actual sales figure is very small, the absolute percentage error can be very large. As we previously saw, a forecast of 6 units will have a percentage error of

−200% if sales turn out to be 2 units. A single sales figure like this can make the MAPE very large, even if most of the other forecasts are quite accurate. Also, like the MPE, the MAPE can't be calculated if one of the sales figures is zero – though some software products get around this by simply ignoring periods when sales are zero.

There are a number of alternatives to the MAPE that attempt to mitigate these problems, which we will discuss in the following sections, but you won't find these measures in all software products.

3.5.2   The Median Absolute Percentage Error (MDAPE)

The MDAPE measure avoids the undue influence that an extremely low or high absolute percentage error can have on our assessment of accuracy. It does this by calculating the median of the absolute errors rather than the mean. For example, suppose that the absolute percentage errors of seven forecasts are as follows:

5%, 14%, 3%, 1%, 9%, 1,000%, 4%

The computer will find the median by ordering the absolute percentage errors from smallest to largest and identifying the middle value. This gives:

1%, 3%, 4%, 5%, 9%, 14%, 1,000%

So the MDAPE is 5%. In contrast, the MAPE would have a value of 148%, which is clearly not typical of any of the percentage errors. Note that the MDAPE would be the same even if the largest error were 100,000%, which shows its robustness to extreme values. If there is an even number of percentage errors, the computer will calculate the median by finding a value that is halfway between the middle two percentage errors. For the forecasts in Table 3.4 the MDAPE is 23.8%, which is almost identical to the MAPE.

3.5.3   The Symmetric Mean Absolute Percentage Error (SMAPE)

Rather than measuring the absolute forecast error as a percentage of the actual sales, the SMAPE first takes the *average* of the forecast and actual sales. It then calculates the error as a percentage of this average: This is referred to as the symmetric absolute percentage error. For example, in Table 3.4, in week 1 we have a forecast of 85 units, but actual sales of 112 units. The average of these two values is 98.5 units. The symmetric absolute percentage error for week 1 is therefore $100 \times 27/98.5 = 27.4\%$. The SMAPE is obtained by taking the mean of the column of symmetric absolute percentage errors. For the forecasts in Table 3.4, this gives a value of 24.1%.

In our case, this is almost the same as the MAPE, but the SMAPE has the advantage that it can be calculated where some of the actual sales are zero – as long as the forecasts for these periods are not also zero. However, some researchers have questioned the appropriateness of the term, symmetric. For example, suppose that actual sales are 100 units. Forecasts of 70 and 130, both 30 units out, would be treated the same by the MAPE. In both cases, the absolute percentage error is 30%. However, the symmetric absolute percentage errors would be $100 \times 30/85 = 35.2\%$ for the first forecast and $100 \times 30/115 = 26.1\%$ for the second. Thus, forecasting 30 units too low is penalized more than forecasting 30 units too high. This might be appropriate in some circumstances, but it could be misleading in others.

3.5.4 The MAD/MEAN Ratio

This measure can be used when some of the sales figures are very small or zero, as in intermittent or low volume demand. The mean absolute error (MAE) or MAD is calculated as shown earlier, and this is then divided by the mean level of sales. The result is expressed as a percentage. For the data in Table 3.3, the MAE we calculated earlier was 24.3 units. The mean level of actual sales over the 15 weeks is 105.3 units, so the MAD/Mean ratio is $100 \times 24.3/105.3 = 23.1\%$.

Researchers have found that this measure offers another advantage over the MAPE. When using an accuracy measure to choose between different forecasting methods, the MAPE can be biased toward methods that produce low forecasts. This is because, if you forecast too low, the worst possible absolute percentage error is 100%. For example, if actual sales are 200 units, the worst underforecast you can make is zero. However, there's no limit to the extent to which you can overforecast, and hence the absolute percentage error for overshooting can be considerably higher than 100%. In contrast, the MAD/Mean ratio does not suffer from this bias.

Note that if we are using the MAD/Mean ratio to measure accuracy for out-of-sample periods, it is usually best to use the mean of the *in-sample* sales in the ratio. This is because we usually have fewer out-of-sample observations, so an estimate of the mean sales based on them is likely to be less reliable. Also, if we have intermittent demand, there's a chance that all of our out-of-sample sales will be zero so, if we used their mean, we couldn't calculate the measure because its denominator would be zero.

3.5.5 Percentage Error Measures When There Is a Trend or Seasonal Pattern

Percentage error measures should be interpreted with care if you have trend or seasonal pattern in your data. If you have an upward trend in your data, the increase in your actual sales will tend to make these measures become smaller over time, giving the impression that forecasts are becoming more accurate even if their typical closeness to actual sales remains the same. The reverse is true for a downward trend. For similar reasons, if you have a seasonal pattern, with sales dipping in the winter and peaking in the summer, your winter sales forecasts will tend to look less accurate than those for the summer.

3.6 RELATIVE ACCURACY MEASURES

There's little point in using a complex and time-consuming forecasting method when a simpler one is more accurate. Even if the simple method is slightly less accurate, the extra effort and expense of the more complex method might not be justified. Relative accuracy measures are designed to allow us to compare the accuracy of a method we are considering using against the benchmark of a simple competitor. Usually, this simple competitor is a naïve forecast – that is, a forecast that equals the most recent sales figure. Sometimes a naïve forecast is referred to as a no-change forecast. Surprisingly, naïve forecasts often outperform much more sophisticated methods.

Like percentage accuracy measures, relative accuracy measures also have the advantage that they are scale free.

3.6.1 Geometric Mean Relative Absolute Error (GMRAE)

Suppose that last week we achieved sales of 53 units. A naïve forecast therefore predicts that next week we will again sell 53 units. However, after we run our computer software, it predicts sales of 70 units for next week. When the actual sales figure arrives, we find that the computer forecast is closest to our actual sales, which turned out to be 80 units. Thus, the computer forecast had an absolute error of 10 units, while the naïve forecast had an absolute error of 27 units.

The ratio of the absolute errors of the two forecasts is called the relative absolute error (RAE) where:

$$\text{RAE} = \frac{\text{Absolute error of our forecast}}{\text{Absolute error of naïve forecast}}$$

In our case, we divide the computer forecast's absolute error by that of the naïve forecast to get $10/27 = 0.37$. This shows that the computer forecast error was less than half that of the naïve forecast. Note that we cannot obtain an RAE if a naïve forecast is perfectly accurate, because we would then be dividing by zero.

When we have several forecasts we can average the RAEs, using the mean or median, to assess the relative accuracy of a method. However, because we are averaging ratios, some software products calculate the geometric mean of the relative absolute errors. The result is referred to as the GMRAE. For example, suppose we have the following seven RAEs for our computer-based forecasts:

$$0.4, \ 1.2, \ 0.6, \ 0.8, \ 1.3, \ 0.2, \ 0.9$$

To calculate their geometric mean, the computer would first multiply the RAEs together to get 0.054. Then, because we have seven values, it would take their seventh root. This gives a GMRAE of 0.66, showing that, typically, our computer-based forecasts have absolute errors that are only 66% of those of naïve forecasts. For our weekly sales example (Table 3.4), it can be shown that the GMRAE is 1.03 suggesting the computer forecasts are slightly less accurate than the naïve forecasts.

We saw earlier that percentage error measures may be misleading where there are trends or seasonal patterns because their denominator involves actual sales. The GMRAE does not have this disadvantage. However, the GMRAE cannot generally be used where demand is intermittent. If we have two consecutive periods with zero sales, the naïve forecast for the second period will be zero, so it will be perfectly accurate and hence have an error of zero. This means we could not calculate the RAE for this period because we would be dividing by zero.

3.6.2 The Mean Absolute Scaled Error (MASE)

The MASE is found by dividing the MAE of our chosen forecasting method by the MAE of naïve forecasts. Table 3.5 shows the calculations

Table 3.5 Calculation of the Mean Absolute Scaled Error (MASE)

Week	No. of Units Sold	Forecasts	Absolute Errors	Naïve Forecasts	Naïve Forecast Absolute Errors
1	112	85			
2	109	88	21	112	3
3	119	90	29	109	10
4	138	93	45	119	19
5	81	98	17	138	57
6	128	96	32	81	47
7	101	99	2	128	27
8	115	99	16	101	14
9	85	101	16	115	30
10	113	99	14	85	28
11	65	100	35	113	48
12	68	97	29	65	3
13	85	94	9	68	17
14	122	93	29	85	37
15	139	96	43	122	17
MAE over periods 2–15			24.1		25.5
MASE			0.94		

of the MASE for our weekly sales example. Because the naïve forecasts are simply the previous week's sales, we don't have a naïve forecast for week 1 so, to make the comparison fair, we have omitted the absolute error of our chosen method from the table for week 1. While our chosen method has an MAE of 24.1, the naïve forecasts have an MAE of 25.5, so the MASE is 24.1/25.5 = 0.94. This suggests that our chosen method is only slightly more accurate than the naïve forecasts.

The MASE, which is a relatively new measure, has a number of advantages. Like the GMRAE, it can be used where there is a trend or seasonal pattern, but it has another benefit – it can usually be used where demand is intermittent. While individual naïve forecasts may be perfectly accurate and have an error of zero, it is very unlikely that the naïve forecasts as a whole will have a *mean* absolute error of zero. Therefore, the problem of dividing by zero, which we saw with the GMRAE, will almost certainly not apply.

Note that if we are using the MASE to measure accuracy for out-of-sample periods, we use the *in-sample* MAE of the naïve forecasts in the denominator. This is because we usually have fewer out-of-sample observations and so, in the case of intermittent demand, there is a high chance that all of the naïve forecasts will forecast zero sales and be perfectly correct. This would mean we couldn't calculate the MASE because we would be dividing by a naïve forecast MAE of zero.

3.6.3 Bayesian Information Criterion (BIC)

Earlier, we noted that you can always find a forecasting formula that will perfectly fit a set of sales figures. To see this, suppose we have the following sales for the last seven weeks:

Week	1	2	3	4	5	6	7
Sales (no. of units)	45	67	63	40	36	51	23

The following formula will fit this sales pattern perfectly:

$$\text{Sales} = 0.0625t^6 - 1.8875t^5 + 20.854t^4 - 106.56t^3$$
$$+ 256.08t^2 - 258.55t + 135$$

where t is the week number. To see this let's put $t = 3$ into the formula. We have:

$$\text{Sales} = 0.00625\,(3)^6 - 1.8875\,(3)^5 + 20.854(3)^4 - 106.56(3)^3$$
$$+ 256.08(3)^2 - 258.55(3) + 135$$

which gives the perfectly correct fit for week 3 of 63 units (subject to rounding). But, if we use the formula to make a forecast for week 8, it predicts that we'll sell minus 151 units!

This is an extreme example of overfitting – of modeling the random movements in the in-sample observations, rather than the underlying pattern that is likely to persist in the future. Clearly, to perfectly fit our seven weeks of sales, we needed quite a complex forecasting formula. Generally, the more complex we make the formula the greater is the danger that our forecasts will suffer from overfitting and be reflecting more of the in-sample noise than they should.

The Bayesian information criterion (BIC), or Schwarz Bayesian information criterion (SBC), balances the aim of getting a good fit to the in-sample sales pattern against the dangers of overfitting. It does this by rewarding a method that has a low mean squared error, while also penalizing it depending on how complex it is. Complexity is measured by the number of parameters that have to be estimated – in our complex model, seven numbers had to be estimated (for brevity, the formula for the BIC has not been included here).

When choosing between different forecast methods, the one with the smallest BIC is usually selected. You may also come across a similar measure, the Akaike information criterion (AIC), which is based on the same principles. This measure penalizes complexity less severely than the BIC.

While these measures are useful in determining which model best represents the underlying pattern in the in-sample data, as always, we must not assume that the indicated method will give the best forecasts – we still need to compare how accurately it forecasts the out-of-sample sales before finally choosing our method.

3.7 COMPARING THE DIFFERENT ACCURACY MEASURES

With so many different accuracy measures available, it's easier to get confused as to which one is appropriate for monitoring your forecasts.

Worse still, the relative accuracy of different methods can vary depending on the accuracy measure used. For example, method A might be best on one accuracy measure but worst on another. Ideally, we should choose the accuracy measure that reflects the costs of forecast errors, such as the loss of customer goodwill resulting from having ordered too few units of a product, or the costs incurred by having too much unsold inventory. However, these costs are usually difficult to calculate.

Fortunately, most forecast software products report more than one accuracy measure enabling you to have a more detailed view of the performance of your forecasts. By studying these, you can gain insights into which of the available forecasting methods is likely to be best for predicting the demand for your products and whether accuracy is improving or deteriorating over time. To help you determine which measures are appropriate in your situation, Table 3.6 summarizes the key attributes of the measures we have discussed.

Table 3.6 Features of Accuracy Measures

Measure	Expressed in Actual Sales Units	Easy to Interpret	Resistant to Freak Sales Figures	Scale Free	Appropriate for Intermittent or Low Volume Sales	Appropriate for Seasonal or Trended Sales	Provides Comparison with Benchmark
MAE	Yes	Yes	No	No	Yes	Yes	No
MSE	No	No	No	No	Yes	Yes	No
RMSE	Yes	No	No	No	Yes	Yes	No
MAPE	No	Yes	No	Yes	No	With care	No
SMAPE	No	No	No	Yes	No	With care	No
MDAPE	No	Yes	Yes	Yes	No	With care	No
MAD/Mean	No	Yes	No	Yes	Yes	No	No
GMRAE	No	No	No	Yes	No	Yes	Yes
MASE	No	Yes	No	Yes	Yes	Yes	Yes
BIC	No	No	No	No	Yes	Yes	No

3.8 EXCEPTION REPORTING

Many companies regularly have to forecast sales for hundreds or thousands of products. In these cases, it would take an inordinate amount of time to continually check the forecast accuracy of every product. Fortunately, some software products have an exception reporting facility that alerts you when the forecasts for a particular product may need your attention. This allows you to focus your time and effort on products where the forecasts may be problematical.

Exception reporting can involve setting up an acceptable range for error measures such as the MAE or MAPE. For example, you can specify that a product should be flagged if its forecasts exceed a MAPE of 40%. You can also ask the software to alert you if the current forecast is predicting an exceptionally large change from what has previously happened in the sales history. For example, you might arrange for an alert if the current forecast for November differs by more than 60% from what we sold last November. Of course, this does not necessarily mean that you'll need to change this forecast, as there might be good reasons for its deviation from last year's figure. Nevertheless, it's worth investigating why this has happened. It might even have resulted from a recent error in data entry.

3.9 FORECAST VALUE-ADDED ANALYSIS (FVA)

We saw earlier that the GMRAE and the MASE automatically compare the accuracy of a method's forecasts with those of naïve forecasts. Since a naïve forecast is about as simple a forecasting method as you can get, these measures therefore give you an indication of whether it's worth going to the effort or cost of employing a more complex method. Mike Gilliland, who is product marketing manager at the SAS Institute, has extended this idea to a process called forecast value-added analysis (FVA).

FVA not only enables you to see whether your forecasting method is more accurate than naïve forecasts, it allows you to examine every step in the forecasting process to see if it is contributing to improved accuracy. For example, suppose that a sales forecasting process in a company involves the following steps:

1. A computer produces a forecast automatically.
2. A sales manager uses her judgment to adjust the forecast based on market intelligence.
3. Senior managers then further adjust the forecast, if they think this is necessary.

The mean absolute percentage errors (MAPEs), based on forecasts for a product over the last 30 weeks, are shown in Table 3.7 for the forecasts produced at the three stages and for naïve forecasts.

It can be seen that the automatic computer forecasts are more accurate than the naïve forecasts – they lower the MAPE by 11 percentage points. Hence the computer's FVA is +11%. The sales manager's judgmental adjustments slightly improve the accuracy of the automatic forecasts – they lower the MAPE by 2 percentage points. However, the senior manager, who finally signs off the forecasts, is damaging accuracy. The adjustments are raising the MAPE by 5 percentage points, so the FVA is −5%.

This analysis suggests that the automatic computer forecasts are performing a useful role. To be sure of this, we would need to compare any costs associated with them (e.g., the cost of renting the software) with the benefits of the extra accuracy. However, although the sales manager's adjustments are improving accuracy, making these adjustments may be time consuming and we would need to assess whether the small FVA of 2% justifies this expenditure of time. It is clear, however, that we should discourage the senior manager from intervening in the process.

FVA has another advantage: It takes into account the predictability of future sales. For example, if we analyze the computerized sales forecasts for two products, we may find that those for Product A have a MAPE of 60% while those for B only have a MAPE of 11%. Because the forecasts for Product A are so inaccurate, we may consider abandoning the computer forecasts for this product and relying on some

Table 3.7 Forecast Value Added (FVA) Analysis

	Naïve Forecasts	Automatic Computer	Sales Manager	Senior Manager
MAPE	32%	21%	19%	24%

other method. However, when we look at the forecast value added by the computer forecasts compared to naïve forecasts, we find that product A has an FVA of 50% while B only has an FVA of 3%. This probably results because the sales of A contain much more random variation and hence are more unpredictable than those of B. So FVA reveals that the computer forecasts are playing a more valuable role in the case of product A than they are for B.

You don't have to use the MAPE when you conduct FVA. As we saw earlier, this measure cannot be calculated when actual sales are zero, and it can have extreme values when actual sales are low. Alternatives include the MAE, MSE, or MDAPE. However, using a relative error measure like the GMRAE or MASE might lead to difficulties of interpretation as these already provide comparisons with naïve forecasts – in fact, they only provide comparisons with naïve forecasts. Also, because they take the form of ratios it might be difficult to assess whether any improvements between methods are justified by the extra costs. You can also apply the method to bias measures to see if bias is improved or worsened at different stages of the forecasting process, or whether naïve forecasts are less biased than a method currently being used.

There are a few caveats to the use of FVA. First, if you want to measure value added across different products, rather than for a single product, then none of the accuracy measures we have met will suffice. For example, you may want to know the average extent to which judgmental adjustments improve accuracy for all of the forecasts for your product range. The problem is that different accuracy metrics can give contradictory results, with some suggesting, for example, that judgmental adjustments are improving accuracy and others that they are reducing it. This can result from a range of problems. For example, some measures may have extreme values for some forecasts (as happens with MAPE when actual sales are low) and so distort the average, while other measures tend to overrate the performance of the benchmark method. If you do want to perform FVA across products, then researchers recommend a measure called the average relative MAE (see the Davydenko and Fildes reference at the end of the chapter). This has not yet been implemented in commercial software.

Second, when you have seasonal sales, the basic naïve forecast is not usually a good benchmark. If sales tend to plummet from August to September, it would not be sensible to use August's sales as a forecast for September. In this case, you can use a seasonal naïve forecast. This simply involves using the sales achieved in the same period last year as the forecast for this year. For example, if we sold 120 units last September, then our seasonal naïve forecast for this September would be 120 units.

Third, we need to be careful before drawing conclusions from FVA that the difference in accuracy between two methods has not arisen by chance. This is particularly true when we have only a few forecasts to compare.

Finally, it's unlikely that your software will have the facility for directly conducting an FVA. In some software products, such as SAS, it's possible to write code that will produce an FVA report, and SAS has produced a white paper that provides this code. Otherwise, you'll have to do the calculations "offline," though they are relatively simple.

3.10 WRAP-UP

1. The performance of a forecasting method should be assessed by comparing its forecasts to sales figures that it has not seen (i.e., the hold-out sample). Assessments based on how well it fits in-sample sales are likely to overestimate how well the method will perform in future.

2. Be aware of the dangers of overfitting.

3. It's important to measure bias in forecasts as well as accuracy.

4. Forecasting software usually reports a variety of bias and accuracy measures. Each has its own advantages and disadvantages, so it is a good idea to use more than one measure to get a more "rounded" view of performance.

5. Take special care when measuring the performance of a method if sales are intermittent.

6. Forecast value-added (FVA) analysis can be useful in identifying which aspects of the forecasting process are damaging performance and which are improving it.

3.11 SUMMARY OF KEY TERMS

In-sample periods.	The section of your sales history that is used to fit a method or model to the data in order to estimate the parameter values that should be used.
Fitted value.	A forecasting method's estimate of what the sales in an in-sample period would be if the effect of noise was removed.
Residual.	The difference between an actual sales value and the fitted value.
Hold-out sample or out-of-sample periods.	The section of your sales history that is reserved for testing how accurately a given method forecasts sales that it has not seen.
Fixed origin evaluation.	A process of fitting and testing a forecasting method where the number of in-sample periods remains fixed.
Rolling-origin evaluation.	A process of fitting and testing a forecasting method where the number of in-sample periods is incremented by one period after forecasts have been tested against the remaining hold-out sample. The procedure is then repeated until no data is left in the hold-out sample.
Overfitting.	A phenomenon where a forecasting method produces forecasts that are too close to the sales in the in-sample periods because it has failed to filter out the noise in these sales.
Forecast error.	Actual sales – Forecast sales.
Absolute error.	A forecast error with any minus sign removed.
Percentage error.	A forecast error expressed as a percentage of actual sales or as a percentage of the average of the forecast and actual sales.
Relative error.	The ratio of a forecasting method's error to that of a benchmark method. Usually the benchmark is a naïve forecast.

Bias.	A persistent tendency for forecasts to be too high or too low.
Naïve forecast.	A forecast that is equal to the most recent sales figure.
Seasonal naïve forecast.	A forecast that is equal to the sales achieved at the same time last year.
Relative accuracy measure.	An accuracy measure that provides a ratio that reflects the accuracy of a forecasting method compared to a benchmark method, such as a naïve forecast.
Bayesian information criterion (BIC).	A measure that reflects the closeness of fitted values to actual sales, but also penalizes more complex methods.
Forecast value-added (FVA) analysis.	A procedure that enables an assessment to be made of the contribution to forecast accuracy of different aspects of the forecasting process. For example, it would allow us to see the extent to which accuracy is improved, or worsened, through judgmental adjustments of computer-generated forecasts, or the use of a complex, rather than a simple, forecasting method.

3.12   REFERENCES

Davydenko, A., and Fildes, R. (2015). Forecast error measures: critical review and practical recommendations. In: M. Gilliland, L. Tashman and U. Sglavo (eds.), *Business Forecasting*. Hoboken, NJ: Wiley.

Hyndman, R. J. (2006). Another look at forecast-accuracy metrics for intermittent demand. *Foresight: The International Journal of Applied Forecasting*, **4**, 43–46.

Kolassa, S., & Schütz, W. (2007). Advantages of the MAD/MEAN ratio over the MAPE. *Foresight: The International Journal of Applied Forecasting*, **6**, 40–43.

Sanders, N. R., & Graman, G. A. (2009). Quantifying costs of forecast errors: A case study of the warehouse environment. *Omega*, **37**, 116–125.

Tashman, L. J. (2000). Out-of-sample tests of forecasting accuracy: an analysis and review. *International Journal of Forecasting*, **16**, 437–450.

CHAPTER **4**

Curve Fitting and Exponential Smoothing

4.1 INTRODUCTION

When you have dedicated forecasting software, you won't have to set up formulae in spreadsheets like Microsoft Excel® or carry out calculations by hand. The software will do the hard work and produce your forecasts as requested. However, it's still worth understanding how these forecasts are obtained so you are aware of the rationale that underpins them. That way you'll have a better understanding of the strengths and limitations of different methods and know whether they are appropriate for your data.

In this chapter, we will look at methods that simply use your sales history to identify and project underlying patterns, such as trends or seasonal cycles, into the future. These methods – called time series methods – don't take any account of factors that might be driving sales, like advertising expenditure or price. Because they only process data on a single variable – past sales – they are referred to as *univariate*, or *time series*, methods. Despite ignoring potential drivers, these methods can be as robust and accurate as methods that are more complex. They also avoid the need to collect and record data on potential drivers, which in some circumstances can be expensive and time consuming. Better still, they can often be run automatically, which is a considerable advantage if you have hundreds or thousands of SKUs to forecast.

Here, we will look at two types of time series methods: those based on fitting curves to the sales history and exponential smoothing. In the following chapter, we will look at a third type of time series method: Box-Jenkins ARIMA models.

4.2 CURVE FITTING

4.2.1 Common Types of Curve

Most forecasting software products have the ability to find a line or curve that best fits a sales history. The idea is to find the underlying trend in the data and to extrapolate this into the future to produce forecasts. Figure 4.1 shows the sales of a product over 20 months. A computer has fitted a curve to the data and, by extending the curve beyond month 20, we can obtain demand forecasts.

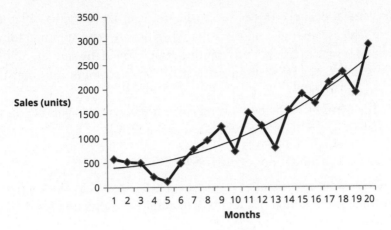

Figure 4.1 Curve fitting

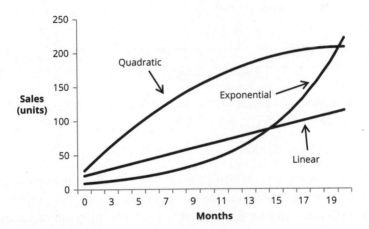

Figure 4.2 Examples of curves

The most common types of curves fitted are: (1) straight lines (for convenience, we'll classify these as a type of curve); (2) quadratic curves; and (3) exponential curves. Figure 4.2 displays an example of these curves. Note that quadratic curves can also have the shape of the fitted curve in Figure 4.1, and, of course, all of the curves can represent downward trends. We'll look at another type of curve, growth curves, when we discuss new product forecasting in Chapter 10.

Computers identify the curve that has the best fit to a sales history by using a procedure called the least squares method. On a sales graph, the vertical distance of each sales figure from the curve is called an error. This is squared, and the squared errors are then summed for all the points on the graph. The resulting total is called the sum of squared errors (SSE). The best-fitting curve is the one that minimizes the sum of squared errors.

The features of the best-fitting curve are described by its equation. A straight line will have an equation of the form:

$$\text{Sales} = a + b \text{ Time}$$

where a and b are numbers, or parameters, estimated by the computer and Time is the period number. For example, the equation for the line in Figure 4.2 is:

$$\text{Sales} = 15 + 5 \text{ Time.}$$

So if want to forecast sales in month 25, we simply substitute 25 for Time in the equation to get: Sales = 15 + 5(25) = 140 units.

A quadratic curve will have an equation of the form:

$$\text{Sales} = a + b \text{ Time} + c \text{ Time}^2$$

where c is also a parameter estimated by the computer. The equation for the quadratic curve in Figure 4.2 is:

$$\text{Sales} = 8 + 20 \text{ Time} - 0.5 \text{ Time}^2.$$

So, for month 25, this curve would forecast Sales = 8 + 20(25) − 0.5(25)^2 = 196 units (after rounding). Note that, by this month, the curve will have passed its peak, so it is now forecasting declining sales.

Finally, exponential curves have equations of the form:

$$\text{Sales} = e^{(a + b \text{ Time})}$$

where e, known as Euler's number, has the approximate value of 2.718. The curve in Figure 4.2 has the equation:

$$\text{Sales} = e^{(2 + 0.17 \text{ Time})}.$$

It would, therefore predict sales of $e^{(2 + 0.17(25))} = 518$ units for month 25.

4.2.2 Assessing How Well the Curve Fits the Sales History

Forecasting software products will normally report a range of measures to tell you how well a curve fits the sales history. These include the MAPE, MAE, and RMSE measures that we met in Chapter 3. But, as we discussed in that chapter, we should be careful not to overfit the data. Remember that more complicated equations will tend to have a better fit to the sales history, but this is likely to be because they are also modeling the noise in the data, and the patterns they identify in noise almost certainly won't be repeated in the future. The BIC measure (also see Chapter 3) can therefore be useful in comparing curves with different levels of complexity, as it penalizes those that have more parameters (e.g., linear equations have just two parameters, a and b, while quadratic equations have three: a, b, and c).

The adjusted R-squared is another measure of fit reported by most software products when fitting curves. This is based on the correlation coefficient, or "r," that we met in Chapter 2. We hope that the forecasts made by our model will be positively correlated with actual sales so that, generally, when our forecasts go up, our sales will also go up and vice versa. So the correlation coefficient gives us some idea of the accuracy of our forecasts. However, it's not a perfect measure of accuracy because it ignores bias in the forecasts. For example, if we make forecasts for the next five weeks of 4, 5, 6, 7, and 8 units, these will be perfectly correlated with actual sales of 14, 15, 16, 17, and 18 units, despite the fact that all of our forecasts are underpredicting sales by 10 units. Nevertheless, if we square the correlation coefficient, we have a measure called R-squared, or the coefficient of determination (unlike the correlation coefficient, this is usually represented by a capital R). For example, if $r = 0.8$, then R-squared $= 0.64$. Clearly, R-squared can only have values between 0 and 1.

So what does R-squared tell us? Usually, the sales in our history will be varying from period to period. For example, the sales in Figure 4.1 have both short-term peaks and troughs, but they also vary in the long run because of the upward trend. R-squared tells us what fraction of this variation is reflected in our fitted curve – technically, what fraction of variation is "explained" by the curve. We can see that the curve in Figure 4.1 reflects much of the long-term variation in sales – the increase in sales from about 500 units to over 2,500 units – but it does not reflect the short-term variations. The computer reveals that the curve has an R-squared of 0.87, so it is not reflecting 13% of the variation in sales. If we had a complex curve that exactly replicated the sales graph in Figure 4.1, then R-squared would be 1 (100% of the variation would be reflected in the curve). If, instead, we fitted a horizontal line through the graph, this would not reflect any of the variation in sales – all our forecasts would be the same – so R-squared would be zero.

As useful as R-squared is, there is a problem. The greater our tendency to overfit the sales history, using more complex curves, the higher it will be. Thus, curves with more parameters tend to have higher R-squared values. To counter this, the *adjusted R*-squared measures how much of the variation in sales is reflected in the curve, while also penalizing curves with more parameters. In this respect, it is similar to the BIC. Like the BIC, it therefore allows curves with different levels of complexity to be compared on a level playing field. For the curve in Figure 4.1 the adjusted R-squared is 0.85 (recall that R-squared was 0.87), so the measure of fit has been slightly reduced because of the three parameters in the curve. If we fitted a straight line to the series, the computer shows that this would have an adjusted R-squared of 0.81, suggesting that the straight line is a slightly poorer model. This is because it isn't able to reflect the curvature in the underlying trend. However, as always, we should not assume that the fit of the curve to past data is a guarantee of future accuracy. Comparing the curves' performances on a hold-out sample would be a much better guide.

4.2.3 Strengths and Limitations of Forecasts Based on Curve Fitting

When we fit a curve to data, and extrapolate it to obtain forecasts, we are said to be using a global model. Global models assume that the underlying trend has the same form across all time periods. For example, a linear equation assumes that underlying sales will always change by the same amount from period to period, while a quadratic curve assumes that the changes in the trend from period to period will always be the same. In practice, as we saw in Chapter 2, the nature of trends can change over time. Fitting a curve to the early sales of a relatively new product, for example, can be misleading, as early sales momentum may not be maintained. Moreover, if we blindly extrapolate a global upward trend into the future, we might find that our sales forecasts are far exceeding the size of the market before too long.

Curve fitting is also not advisable where you have seasonal patterns in your data. The estimates of the best-fitting curve can be sensitive to the sales at the start and end of the sales history, because they have what is referred to as leverage. Hence, a sales history that ends on a high summer peak may lead to the estimation of a different curve than a history that ends in a winter trough.

While curve fitting is simple to implement, it can be seen that it has a number of disadvantages as a forecasting method. In particular, it can't take into account changing patterns in trends in the past or in the future. It should therefore only be used with care, and it's always a good idea to apply a sanity check to any trends it identifies. Is it plausible that sales will go on increasing or decreasing at the rate it suggests? Are we in danger of forecasting negative sales when we extrapolate the curve?

In the next section, we discuss some widely used methods that can handle changes in the pattern of sales over time. They do this by revising their estimates of what is happening as each new sales figure arrives.

4.3 EXPONENTIAL SMOOTHING METHODS

4.3.1 Simple (or Single) Exponential Smoothing

Simple exponential smoothing (SES) is appropriate when the sales history does not have a trend or seasonal pattern, but the underlying level of sales can change. For example, it may suddenly step upward by 10 units and stay at that level for a few weeks, before stepping down by 6 units, and so on. Of course, actual sales will vary randomly around the current level, so the task of SES is to estimate what that level is.

Table 4.1   Simple Exponential Smoothing

Week	Sales	Forecast	Error	0.2 × Error	Next Forecast
1	65	45	20	4	49
2	39	49	−10	−2	47
3	57	47	10	2	49
4	79	49	30	6	55
5	35	55	−20	−4	51
6	46	51	−5	−1	50
7	60	50	10	2	52
8		52			
9		52			
10		52			

On receiving each new sales figure, SES revises its estimate of the level. It then projects this level forward to produce its forecasts.

Table 4.1 shows the sales of a product over seven weeks. These sales are also displayed in Figure 4.3. To start SES you need an initial forecast for week 1. This will be estimated automatically by the computer. In our case, as shown in Table 4.1, this is 45 units. When the sales figure for week 1 is available, it turns out to be 65 units, so the initial forecast had an error of 65 − 45 = 20 units. Because we underforecasted by 20 units, this might be a sign that the underlying level of sales is higher. However, this might also be due to noise. In our case, SES tries

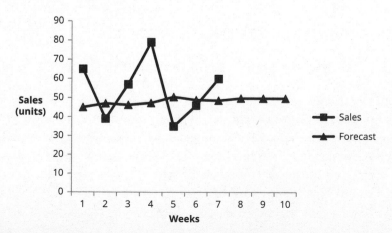

Figure 4.3   Sales and simple exponential smoothing forecasts

to balance these possibilities by increasing its previous forecast by just 20% or 0.2 of the error. This means its forecast for week 2 is 45 + 0.2 × 20 = 49 units. The 0.2 is called the smoothing constant, and it can be any value between 0 and 1. Larger smoothing constants mean that more attention is paid to the latest forecast error, leading to a bigger change from the forecast for the previous period.

When the week 2 sales figure of 39 units is available, we find that our forecast of 49 units had an error of 39 − 49 = −10 units, so this time we forecast too high. In the light of this, we adjust the previous forecast downwards to get a forecast for week 3 of 49 + 0.2 × (−10) = 47 units. The process continues in the same way, as shown in Table 4.1.

Because SES assumes that there is no trend in sales, forecasts for more than one-period ahead are the same as the one-period-ahead forecast (i.e., a flat line is projected forward). In Table 4.1 we only have sales data for the first seven weeks, so forecasts for weeks 8, 9, and 10 are all equal to 52 units. This may appear simplistic, but these forecasts may be reliable. In particular, we should remember that we are not trying to forecast the future noise that may be associated with sales in weeks 8 to 10. Figure 4.3 shows how SES has smoothed out the series in its quest to filter out the noise in the sales history and identify the underlying level at each point in time.

How do we determine the "best" value of the smoothing constant? Most software packages automatically find the value that minimizes the mean squared error (MSE) of the forecasts over the available sales history. In our case, using a smoothing constant of 0.2 we have an MSE = $[20^2 + (−10)^2 + \ldots\ldots + (−5)^2 + 10^2]/7 = 289.3$. It can be shown that a smoothing constant of 0.099 would lead to the lowest MSE of 280.5. Of course, seven sales figures is a small sample, so our estimate of the "best" smoothing constant may be unreliable and, ideally, we should base it on a longer sales history. We should also test how well forecasts based on this smoothing constant perform on a hold-out sample.

Most software packages give you the opportunity to set the smoothing constant manually. What is the effect of increasing or reducing this constant? The SES forecasting formula we used above was:

Forecast for next period = Current forecast + α Forecast error

= Current forecast + α (Latest sales − Current forecast)

where α (alpha) is the smoothing constant.

The above formula can be rewritten as:

Forecast for next period = α Latest sales + $(1 - \alpha)$ Current forecast

It can be seen that the forecast for the next period is a weighted average of the latest sales and the current forecast. If you increase the smoothing constant, your forecast will give more weight to the latest sales figure. This will make it more sensitive to possible changes in the underlying level of sales so it will pick these up quicker. However, this also makes your forecast more vulnerable to being fooled by random movements in sales. Ultimately, if you increase the smoothing constant to its maximum value of 1, then each forecast will simply be equal to the latest sales figure, so it will be a naïve forecast.

If, instead, you decrease the smoothing constant, the forecast places less weight on the latest sales figure and hence is more stable – it will tend to discount much of the variation in sales simply as noise. However, when there is a genuine change in the underlying sales level, it will take many periods before the forecasts adjust to the new level. If you choose a smoothing constant of zero, all of the forecasts will be the same as the initial forecast, and they will not change, whatever is happening to sales. It's difficult to think of circumstances where this would be sensible.

4.3.2 Exponential Smoothing When There Is a Trend: Holt's Method

If there's a trend in sales, then simple exponential smoothing will always forecast too low if the trend is upward, or too high if it's downward. The forecasts will never catch up with the actual sales. What we need is a method that can cope with a trend and also detect changes in the trend as time moves on. When the trend is linear, Holt's method meets these requirements.

The method works on the same principles as SES, but when it receives the latest sales figure, it updates two estimates: (1) Its estimate of the underlying level of sales at the current time; and (2) its estimate of the current trend (i.e., the expected change in the level between now and the next period). To perform these two updates, Holt's method has two smoothing constants – one for updating the level estimate and the other for updating the estimate of the trend. The computer usually chooses the pair of values that minimizes the mean squared error over the sales history.

This is how Holt's method produces a forecast once the latest sales figure is known.

1. *It updates its estimate of the underlying level of sales at the current period using the following formula.*

   Current estimate of level = α Latest sales + $(1 - \alpha)$

   $\times$ (previous estimate of level + previous estimate of trend)

   Suppose that last week we thought that the underlying level of sales was 47 units and we thought that there was a trend – the underlying sales level appeared to increasing by 3 units a week. This means we would expect that the underlying level this week will be $47 + 3 = 50$ units. However, this week's sales turn out to be 60 units – more than we expected. This could be a freak result or it could be a signal that sales are now increasing at a faster rate. To balance these possibilities, Holt's method takes a weighted average of what the latest sales figure suggests and what it originally expected the level to be. For example, if $\alpha = 0.1$, the current estimate of the level will be: $0.1(60) + 0.9(50) = 51$ units.

2. *The next step is to update the estimate of the trend.* In Holt's method the smoothing constant for the trend is usually represented by β (beta), which is also always between 0 and 1. Having a second smoothing constant allows us to have different degrees of responsiveness to changing levels and to changing trends.

   The formula for updating the trend estimate is:

   Current estimate of trend = β (Latest observation of trend)

   $+ (1 - \beta)$ Previous estimate of trend

   Our latest observation of the trend will be the difference between last week's level estimate and this week's. We estimated the underlying level last week to be 47 units. From stage 1, this week's level is estimated to be 51 units – this suggests an upward trend of four units per week. Last week, we thought the trend was 3 units. Consistent with the principle of exponential smoothing, we take a weighted average of the two trend estimates. For example, if $\beta = 0.2$, our current estimate of the trend will be: $0.2(4) + 0.8(3) = 3.2$ units. The higher than expected sales figure has made us slightly increase our estimate of the rate at which underlying sales are increasing.

3. To make a forecast for the next period we simply add our current level estimate to our current trend estimate. Our forecast for next week's sales will therefore be: $51 + 3.2 = 54.2$ units. The software might round this to 54 units, but a forecast of 54.2 units is sensible. Remember that point forecasts are predicting the mean level of demand in a future period – the average of the possible levels of demand in a future period, after taking into account their probabilities – and an average does not have to be a whole number.

   Since we currently think that underlying sales are increasing by 3.2 units per week, our forecast for two weeks ahead will be $51 + 2(3.2) = 57.4$ units and so on. We simply add the appropriate multiple of the trend to our current level estimate. This shows that Holt's method assumes that the trend is linear. In our case, it assumes that underlying sales will go on increasing at the rate of 3.2 units per week into the future.

Like simple exponential smoothing, Holt's method requires forecasting software to produce initial estimates of the level and trend. You may find that your software offers an alternative to Holt's method called Brown's double exponential smoothing. This is a special case of Holt's method when $\alpha = \beta$. When a very large number of forecasts need to be made regularly, this has the advantage that the computer needs only to optimize one parameter for each sales history, rather than two. Neither Holt's nor Brown's method is suitable where sales have a seasonal pattern, unless the data have first been deseasonalized, as they would confuse seasonal movements with a changing trend.

4.3.3 The Damped Holt's Method

As we have seen, because Holt's method assumes a linear trend, its forecasts imply that sales will go on increasing, or decreasing, at the same rate forever. In practice, this is unlikely, especially in the longer term, as extra sales become harder and harder to achieve. This means that when there is an upward trend, Holt's method tends to produce forecasts that are too high when forecasting several periods ahead. This limitation led to the development of the damped Holt's method. It projects a trend that is gradually slowing down and ultimately approaches a horizontal line on a sales graph. The method has been found to be accurate, compared to other trend forecasting methods, and is widely used.

The damping is achieved by introducing a third parameter, φ (theta), which has a value between 0 and 1. When $\varphi = 1$, the forecasts are not damped at all, so they are the same as those produced by the "basic" Holt's method. The smaller the value of φ, then the greater will be the amount of damping. As before, forecasting software will usually attempt to determine the best value of φ by finding the values of α, β, and φ that minimize the MSE over the available sales history. (Note that the updating equations for the damped Holt's method are slightly different from those of the basic method, but for brevity are not presented here.)

If our current estimate of the underlying level of sales is 200 units and the current trend estimate is 10 units, Holts' method would produce forecasts of 210, 220, 230 units, and so on for one, two, and three periods ahead, respectively. If we have $\varphi = 0.7$, the damped Holt's method would produce its forecasts as follows:

Forecast for next period $= 200 + 0.7(10) = 207$ units

The two-period-ahead forecast would be: $200 + 0.7(10)$
$+ 0.7^2(10) = 211.9$ units

The three-period-ahead forecast would be: $200 + 0.7(10)$
$+ 0.7^2(10) + 0.7^3(10) = 215.3$ units

This pattern of forecasting continues in the same way for longer lead times. Figure 4.4 compares the forecasts for up to 10 periods ahead, using Holt's method and the damped Holt's method with φ values of 0.7 or 0.9.

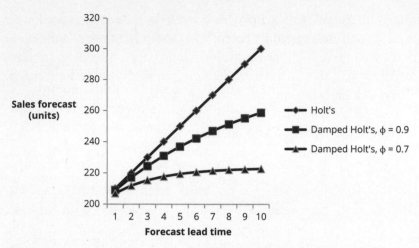

Figure 4.4 Forecasts produced by Holt's method and the damped Holt's method

4.3.4   Holt's Method with an Exponential Trend

When sales are following an exponential trend, this means that the trend is itself changing at a constant rate. For example, a linear trend might involve underlying sales increasing by 3 units per month. Our underlying sales might therefore be 100, 103, 106, and 109 units in successive months. When the trend is exponential, each successive underlying sales level might be 10% greater (i.e., 1.1 times) the previous level. Successive levels might therefore be 100, 110, 121, 133.1, and 146.4 units. In this case, Holt's method takes the ratio of successive levels (1.1 in this case) as an estimate of the current growth rate. It then produces its forecasts by using the following formula:

Forecast for h periods ahead = Current level estimate

$$\times\ (\text{Current growth rate estimate})^h$$

For example, if our current level estimate is 200 units and our current growth rate estimate is 1.2 units, then a one-period-ahead forecast would be: $200(1.2)^1 = 240$ units. The two period ahead forecast would be: $200(1.2)^2 = 288$ units, and so on. (Note that the updating equations for Holt's method with an exponential trend are different from those of the "basic" method, but again for brevity these are not presented here.)

4.3.5 Exponential Smoothing Where There Is a Trend and Seasonal Pattern: The Holt-Winters Method

When there is a seasonal pattern in sales, this also can be subject to change as time goes on. For example, a food or drink product may become more fashionable at Christmas. Or summer clothes may see increasing sales in the winter as more consumers take winter holidays abroad in a warmer climate. The Holt-Winters method produces forecasts when there is a trend and seasonal pattern in sales, and where both are subject to change over time.

Holt-Winters is an extension of Holt's method. In addition to updating its estimate of the underlying level of sales and the trend, it also updates its estimate of the seasonal pattern as soon as the latest sales figure is available. It does this using a third smoothing constant, γ (gamma), which is also always between 0 and 1. As we saw in Chapter 2, seasonal patterns can be additive or multiplicative and there is a form of the Holt-Winters method for each type of pattern.

For example, suppose that we have an additive seasonal pattern and have just received the sales figure for June. A year ago, the method estimated that the seasonal index for June was +120 units, suggesting that June's sales tend to be 120 units above the underlying level of sales. However, this June, sales are only 80 units above the expected underlying level for that month. As before, we take a weighted average of the information based on latest sales figure and our previous estimate of June's seasonal index. If γ is 0.2, our updated estimate of June's seasonal index would be: $0.2(80) + 0.8(120) = 112$ units. The disappointing sales figure for June has caused us to reduce our estimate of the extent to which its sales are expected to exceed the underlying level.

If, instead, the seasonal pattern was multiplicative, the Holt-Winter's method would use a similar procedure, but this time the seasonal indices would be expressed as ratios to the underlying level (see Chapter 2). For example, if last year June's seasonal index was estimated to be 1.30 (suggesting that June's sales could be expected to be 30% above the underlying level) but this June's sales figure is only 10% above the underlying level, our new seasonal index for June would be: $0.2(1.1) + 0.8(1.3) = 1.26$.

Of course, we won't use our new estimate of June's seasonal index until we need to make a forecast for next June. If we now want to make a forecast for July of this year, we will be using our latest estimates of the level and trend, but a seasonal index that was estimated 11 months ago in July last year. If, say, we have an additive seasonal pattern, and after receiving June's sales figure, we have a level estimate of 400, a trend estimate of 6, and the seasonal index for July is + 70, our forecast for July will be:

Latest level estimate + Latest trend estimate + July seasonal index

$$= 400 + 6 + 70 = 476 \text{ units.}$$

If the seasonal pattern is multiplicative and the seasonal index for July is 1.1, then our forecast for July will be:

(Latest level estimate + Latest trend estimate) × July seasonal index

$$= (400 + 6)\, 1.1 = 447 \text{ units.}$$

Because the seasonal indices for a particular month or quarter are only updated once a year, they are often based on relatively few observations. For example, if you have three years of monthly data, the computer will have to estimate June's seasonal index based on only three June sales figures. In these cases, the estimates need to be viewed with caution, as the computer will not have had much chance to filter out noise from them, and research suggests that they may tend to exaggerate the amount of variation in sales caused by seasonality.

4.3.6 Overview of Exponential Smoothing Methods

Table 4.2 shows the variety of exponential smoothing methods that can be available in forecasting software. In many packages, if you wish, you can ask the software to determine automatically the method that it thinks is most appropriate. We will weigh the advantages of manual versus automatic selection in Chapter 8.

4.4 FORECASTING INTERMITTENT DEMAND

When demand is intermittent, so that periods when sales are made are interspersed with periods of zero sales, simple exponential smoothing

Table 4.2 Available Exponential Smoothing Methods

Trend	None	Seasonality Additive	Multiplicative
None	SES	HW additive seasonality with initial trend & $\beta = 0$	HW multiplicative seasonality with initial trend & $\beta = 0$
Linear	Holt's	HW additive seasonality, linear trend	HW multiplicative seasonality, linear trend
Damped	Damped Holt's	HW additive seasonality, damped trend	HW multiplicative seasonality, damped trend
Exponential	Holt's with exponential trend	HW additive seasonality, exponential trend	HW multiplicative seasonality, exponential trend

HW = Holt-Winters method

Table 4.3 Simple Exponential Smoothing and Intermittent Demand

Month	Jun	Jul	Aug	Sep	Oct
Sales (units)	4	0	1	0	0
SES forecasts	1	2.20	1.32	1.19	0.72

(SES) does not perform well. Consider the demand history in Table 4.3. This shows sales over five months for a product that has intermittent demand.

Suppose that, unknown to the forecaster, the true mean monthly demand for this product, averaged over all months, is just 0.5 units (e.g., typically we sell 1 unit every two periods on average). SES with a smoothing constant of 0.4 is now being used to forecast the mean demand, and the forecast of mean demand it has for June is 1 unit. Table 4.3 shows what happens after we have a demand of 4 units in June. The subsequent forecast for July has gone up to 2.20 units – so the method is now forecasting a mean that is far too high. The problem is that we are most likely to place an order for new stock at this point – when we have just sold several units of the product. Our stock of the product has been reduced and may, by now, have dwindled to the point where we think that new supplies are needed. If, for example, we order 12 months supplies at once, we would base our reorder decision on the SES forecast. This suggests an expected demand over the year of $12 \times 2.2 = 26.4$ units, when the true expect demand is only $0.5 \times 12 = 6$ units. Holding this amount of excessive stock can be costly if the product is expensive to buy and store.

SES therefore tends to overestimate mean demand just after a period when sales have been made. To try to address this problem, the statistician John Croston developed an alternative method that is now available for forecasting intermittent demand in many software products. Croston's method involves making two separate forecasts: One for the mean interval between periods when we have demand and one for the mean size of demand in periods when we do have a demand. This is how the method works.

1. If you have demand in a period:
   a. Update the forecast of the mean size of demand using SES. In Table 4.3, as we've seen, this give a forecast of 2.2 units after June's demand figure is known.
   b. Use SES to revise the forecast of the mean interval between periods when we have a demand.

      Suppose that, prior to June, when we last had a demand, we made a forecast that the mean interval between demand periods would be four months. However, when we had a demand in June, it was only two months since there was a previous demand for the product. Using a smoothing constant of 0.4, our revised forecast of the mean interval would be:

      $$0.4(2) + 0.6(4) = 3.2 \text{ months.}$$

   c. The new forecast of mean demand
      $$= \frac{\text{Forecast of mean demand size}}{\text{Forecast of mean interval}}$$

   For our example, this gives a forecast of mean demand = $2.2/3.2 = 0.69$ units per month.

2. If you do not have demand in a period, leave all of your forecasts the same.

The process would now continue in the same way for the months following June. Note that the choice of a smoothing constant of 0.4

in our example was merely to illustrate the method, and, in practice, smaller values are likely to be used.

Although Croston's method reduces the tendency of SES to produce forecasts of mean demand that are too high, researchers have found that it does not completely eliminate this bias. One solution is to modify the Croston forecast using the Syntetos-Boylan correction. This has not been generally implemented in software products, so the correction would need to be carried out offline by using the following simple formula:

$$\text{Modified forecast} = (1 - \alpha/2) \text{ Croston forecast}$$

In our example, we would therefore have: Modified forecast = $(1 - 0.4/2)0.69 = 0.55$ units. Even the corrected forecasts are still likely to be slightly biased (in this case they tend to be a little bit too low), but they represent an appreciable improvement on the Croston forecasts. Other variants of Croston's method are available in some software products.

4.5 WRAP-UP

1. Curve fitting is a relatively simple way to produce forecasts of the underlying trend in sales, but its assumption of a global trend means that it cannot react to changing conditions. In particular, long-range forecasts based on this method are likely to be inaccurate. Use of the method is also not advisable when a sales history has a seasonal pattern.

2. Exponential smoothing methods do allow forecasts to adapt to changing conditions as the latest sales figures become available, and different forms of the method have been developed for untrended, trended, and seasonal sales and also for situations where demand is intermittent. The methods are simple to implement, and there is evidence that they often produce forecasts that are more accurate than more complex methods. In particular, they can be easily automated, which is useful when a large number of forecasts need to be made on a regular basis.

3. None of the methods in this chapter provides explanations of why sales are increasing or decreasing. For example, they do not tell us whether variations in sales are linked to factors such as changes in price or weather conditions. Their forecasts are simply extrapolations of underlying patterns that have been detected in the sales history.

4.6 SUMMARY OF KEY TERMS

R-squared. Also known as the coefficient of determination. A measure of the proportion of variation in actual sales over time that is reflected in the fitted values of a forecasting method. It has a value that falls on a scale between 0 and 1 or between 0 and 100%.

Adjusted R-squared. An *R*-squared value that is adjusted so that it penalizes forecasting models that have more parameters. This allows the fit of models with different levels of complexity to be compared on equal terms.

Global model. A forecasting model that assumes that the nature of features, such as the trend or seasonal pattern, will not change over time.

Exponential smoothing. A collection of forecasting methods that update their estimates of the current level, trend, or seasonal pattern when the latest sales figure is available.

Smoothing constant. A number between 0 and 1 that determines how big a change is made to the estimate of the current level, trend, or seasonal pattern when the latest sales figure is received.

Simple exponential smoothing (SES). Also known as single exponential smoothing. A type of exponential smoothing that updates its estimate of the underlying level of sales when the latest sales figure is received.

Holt's method.	A type of exponential smoothing that updates its estimate of both the underlying level of sales and the trend when the latest sales figure is received. It uses different smoothing constants for the level and trend and assumes a linear trend.
Damped Holt's method.	An extension of Holt's method that projects a damped trend into the future to produce its forecasts. A third parameter is used to determine the degree of damping.
Double exponential smoothing.	A special case of Holt's method that uses the same smoothing constant for updating the estimates of the level and trend.
Holt-Winters method.	Also sometimes called Winters method. A type of exponential smoothing that updates its estimate of the underlying level of sales, the trend, and the seasonal pattern when the latest sales figure is received. It uses different smoothing constants for the level, trend, and seasonal pattern.
Croston's method.	A special form of exponential smoothing designed to forecast average demand when sales are intermittent.
Syntetos-Boylan correction.	A factor that can be applied to forecasts from Croston's method to reduce the upwards bias of its forecasts.

CHAPTER **5**

Box-Jenkins
ARIMA Models

5.1 INTRODUCTION

The Box-Jenkins method is a relatively advanced approach to short-term forecasting that exploits the autocorrelations between observations at different points in time to produce forecasts. Like exponential smoothing, it is a univariate method, so it only uses data in the sales history to produce its forecasts. The method involves a formal series of steps, which include identifying a tentative model and then using a battery of diagnostic tests to assess the model's adequacy. However, some software packages will automatically identify and fit the most appropriate model for you. Later, we will look at why Box-Jenkins models are also called ARMA or ARIMA models; but first, we'll explore the models that are appropriate when we have a sales history that is described as stationary.

5.2 STATIONARITY

Stationary time series are sales histories that have an underlying structure that does not change over time. For example, their underlying mean and their variability remain the same. There are a number of ways of assessing whether series are stationary, but we can gain an initial idea by looking at the graph of the series. In Figure 5.1, the upward-sloping series is nonstationary – clearly, the mean level of sales gets larger over time. The "flat" series is stationary – the underlying mean level of sales does not change over time. The series in Figure 5.2 is not stationary. Its underlying mean is the same, but its variability increases over time. It is said to be nonstationary in the variance.

However, graphs like this can be deceiving. For example, a graph may appear to be generally flat, but there may be changes in the underlying mean that are difficult to detect – such as where the sales occasionally step up or down to slightly higher or lower levels. A better way of detecting when the mean of a series is nonstationary is to ask the computer to plot an autocorrelation function (or ACF) (see Chapter 2). Recall that this shows the correlation between sales that are 1, 2, 3, 4..., etc. periods apart. The typical ACF for a nonstationary series is shown in Figure 5.3. Notice how it declines very slowly as the lag increases. Above average sales tend to be followed by other above

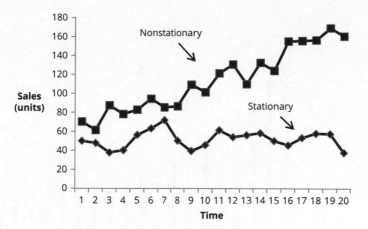

Figure 5.1 Stationary and nonstationary series

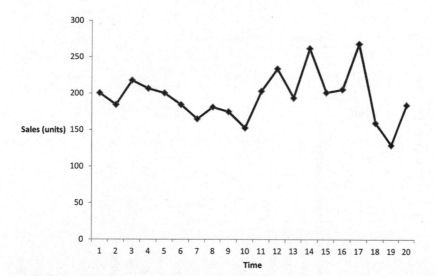

Figure 5.2 A series that has a nonstationary variance

average sales even if they are a large number of periods apart and vice versa. Contrast this with the ACF for the stationary series shown in Figure 5.4. The large autocorrelations disappear much more rapidly as the lags increase, and after a very few lags, they are mostly close to zero. Note that the autocorrelations can be positive and negative, and it is their absolute size that we should be considering when assessing stationarity.

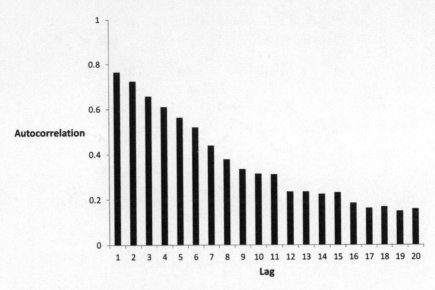

Figure 5.3 An ACF for a series that has a nonstationary mean

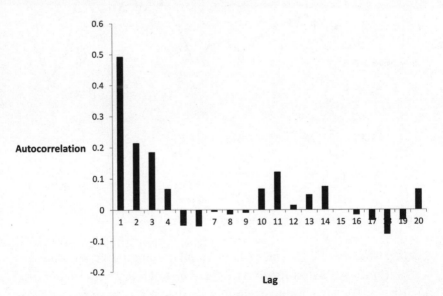

Figure 5.4 An ACF for a series that has a stationary mean

5.3 MODELS OF STATIONARY TIME SERIES: AUTOREGRESSIVE MODELS

In the Box-Jenkins method, two types of model are available for stationary series: Autoregressive and moving average models. Collectively, these are called ARMA or autoregressive moving average models.

The simplest autoregressive model has the form:

Sales in a given period = $a + b$ Sales in previous period + Noise

where a and b are parameters estimated by the computer. For example, a sales history might be represented by the following model:

Sales in a given week = 200 + 0.63 Sales in previous week + Noise

If we have sales this week of 520 units, we will forecast sales next week of 200 + 0.63(520) = 528 units. The model suggests that, if we had relatively high sales this week, we can expect relatively high sales next week, and vice versa. Of course, actual sales are likely to differ from the forecast because of noise. This is known as a first-order autoregressive model because it only models the relationship between sales one period apart.

A second-order autoregressive model has the form:

Sales in a given period = $a + b_1$ Sales in previous period

$+ b_2$ Sales two periods previously + Noise

For example, the computer might fit the following model to a sales history:

Sales in a given week = 50 − 0.3 Sales in previous week

+ 0.4 Sales two weeks previously + Noise

If necessary, we could go on extending autoregressive models to include sales that occurred more than two periods back.

How do we know whether an autoregressive model is likely to be suitable for forecasting the sales of a particular product? The answer is that we can study the patterns in the ACF and an associated graph, the partial autocorrelation function, or PACF. Partial autocorrelation is a measure of the correlation between sales that are a given number of periods apart, when the effect of sales in the intervening weeks

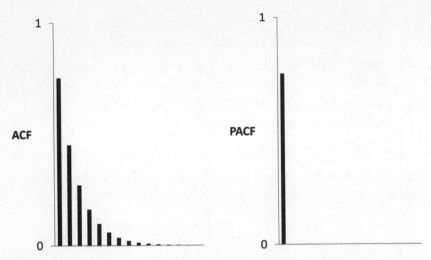

Figure 5.5 Theoretical ACF and PACF for a first-order autoregressive model

has been removed. A first-order autoregressive model should, in theory, have patterns like those shown in Figure 5.5. This shows a quick decline in the ACF and one significant spike at a lag of one period for the PACF. The ACF for the first order autoregressive model shows that sales in a given period are correlated, not only with those of the previous period, but also, to a lesser extent, with those two periods earlier and those three periods earlier, and so on. The more distant the earlier period the less will be its correlation with current sales, but the model suggests that exceptionally high or low sales in any period will have an impact on subsequent sales for some time to come.

For a second-order autoregressive model there would be spikes in the PACF at lags of both one and two periods and so on for higher order models. Note again that it is the absolute size of the bars in the graphs that we should be considering, not their sign. Where we have negative autocorrelations, some, or all, of the bars will appear below the horizontal axis.

In practice, the actual ACF and PACFs rarely conform exactly to the theoretical patterns, like those shown in Figure 5.5, and deciding whether an autoregressive model is appropriate can be a judgment call. However, some commercial software products provide an expert system that will automatically identify the model it thinks is most appropriate. Also, at this stage in the application of the Box-Jenkins method, the model is only provisional and a series of diagnostic tests is available later to help you to assess whether it is appropriate. We will look at the merits of allowing the computer to choose a model automatically in Chapter 8.

5.4 MODELS OF STATIONARY TIME SERIES: MOVING AVERAGE MODELS

Moving average models show the relationship between the sales in a given period and random events, or shocks, in earlier periods. For example, suppose that last week people bought less of our product than expected because of poor weather conditions. This week, we might expect higher than average sales as people buy what they originally intended to purchase last week. The use of the term *moving average* here should not be confused with the idea of a simple average that is updated over time.

The most straightforward moving average model has the form:

Sales in a given period = $a + b$ Noise in previous period + Noise

For example, a model might look like:

Sales in a given period = $130 - 0.42$ Noise in previous period + Noise

The error in the forecast for the previous period is used as the estimate of noise for that period. Suppose that last week's forecast had an error of 12 units. In this case, our forecast of this week's sales would be: $130 - 0.42(12) = 125$ units. Of course the actual sales are likely to deviate from the forecasts because of noise that we can't predict. This relatively simple model is known as a first-order moving average model. A second-order moving average model would have the following form:

Sales in a given period = $a + b_1$ Noise in previous period

$+ b_2$ Noise two periods previously + Noise

If a first-order moving average is appropriate for a time series, in theory its ACF and PACF will look like those in Figure 5.6. This is exactly the reverse of the pattern we would expect for the first-order autoregressive model – the ACF and PACF patterns have been interchanged. It can be seen that the ACF consists of a single spike in the

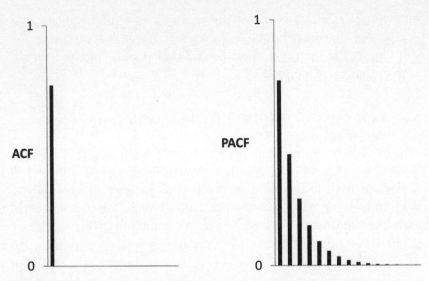

Figure 5.6 Theoretical ACF and PACF for a first-order moving average model

autocorrelation function at lag 1, but zero autocorrelations thereafter. Thus, the first-order model assumes that sales in each period are correlated with sales in the previous period, but not with any earlier sales. This contrasts with the first-order autoregressive model. For a second-order moving average model we would expect two significant spikes in the ACF and so on for higher-order models. Once again, note that some of the bars are likely to be negative, but it is their absolute sizes that are of interest.

5.5 MODELS OF STATIONARY TIME SERIES: MIXED MODELS

Sometimes an appropriate forecasting model has both autoregressive and moving average terms. For example, a computer might fit the following model to a sales history:

Sales in a given period = 130 + 0.21 Sales in previous period

— 0.42 Noise in previous period + Noise

This would be an example of a first-order autoregressive moving average model. When a mixed model is appropriate theoretically, *both* the ACF and PACF decline to zero, showing the same pattern as the right-hand graph of Figure 5.6.

5.6   FITTING A MODEL TO A STATIONARY TIME SERIES

Figure 5.7 shows the sales of a product over 50 weeks. Figure 5.8 shows the ACF and PACF for the series.

The graphs suggest that the series is stationary. The single long spike at lag 1 in the ACF and the quick decline in the PACF over the first three lags are consistent with a first-order moving average model. The other spikes in the graph are of some concern, but they are smaller and are probably due to chance. If our judgment is wrong, the diagnostic tests we perform later should indicate this.

We can now use forecasting software to find the first-order moving average model that best fits the historic series. Table 5.1 shows a typical

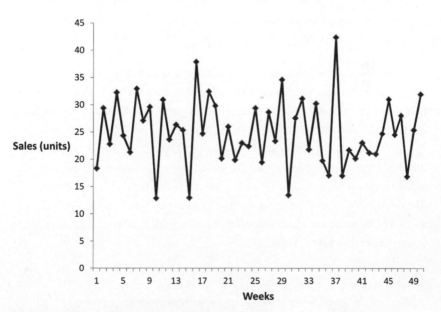

Figure 5.7   Sales of a product over 50 weeks

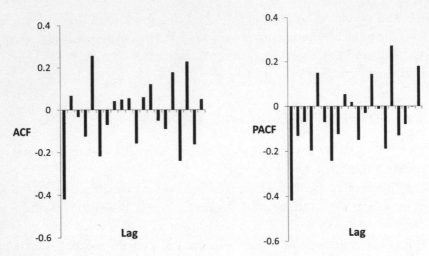

Figure 5.8 ACF and PACF for example product

computer presentation of the results. The constant is a in our models, and the MA1 term is b. This indicates that the best fitting model is:

$$\text{Sales in a given week} = 25.02 - 0.5176$$
$$\times \text{Noise in previous period} + \text{Noise}$$

If we asked the computer to display the forecast error for the most recent month, month 50, we would see this was 5.50 units. So, using this error as the estimate of noise in the previous month, the forecast for week 51 would be: $25.02 - 0.5176 \times 5.50 = 22.17$ units. If we wish to use our model to forecast two months ahead, we have a problem – we don't yet have the sales figure for month 51, so we can't know the error in our forecast. The best we can do is assume that the error, and hence the noise, will be zero, so our forecast will be: $25.02 - 0.5176(0) = 25.02$ units. In fact, the forecasts made for all lead times greater than 1 will have this same value.

Table 5.1 Estimation of Best-Fitting Moving Average Model

Term	Coefficient	Standard Error	t-Statistic	p-Value
Constant	25.0194	0.3856	64.89	0.000
MA1	−0.5176	0.1237	−4.18	0.000

We found the same issue occurred with simple exponential smoothing (SES) forecasts in Chapter 4, so both methods are generally only useful for very short-term forecasting.

5.7 DIAGNOSTIC CHECKS

Before we can be confident in using our model for forecasting, we need to perform four diagnostic checks.

5.7.1 Check 1: Are the Coefficients of the Model Statistically Significant?

There is a danger, particularly where data histories are short, that we will be misled by chance patterns in our data and will see autocorrelations when really the series is totally random. To guard against this, we carry out significance tests on our model. The key numbers in Table 5.1 are the p-values. Notice that sometimes these are labeled "Significance" and some software products display $1 - p$ instead, so you will need to check your package's documentation. A p-value shows the probability of an estimated coefficient having a value as far from zero as it is if its true value is really zero. For example, if the true value of the constant is zero, the probability of getting an estimate of 25.02 or more is virtually 0 (it won't be quite 0 – the software has rounded the very small probability to four decimal places). Similarly, if the true moving average coefficient of the model is zero, the probability of obtaining an estimate of –0.5176 or less is also virtually 0. It therefore appears to be very unlikely indeed that our results have simply arisen by chance. For both the constant and the moving average coefficient, we can therefore reject a hypothesis that its true value is zero.

How low do the p-values have to be before we can reject a hypothesis that a coefficient has a true value of zero? Conventionally, it is rejected when a p-value is less than 0.05. In this case, the coefficient is said to be statistically significant. Note that the standard error and t-statistic columns in Table 5.1 underpin the calculation of the p-values, so we will not interpret them here.

5.7.2 Check 2: Overfitting—Should We Be Using a More Complex Model?

We want our model to represent the entire systematic pattern in the sales history. There may be elements of this pattern that our model has missed. To check this, we can fit more complex models to the data and see if their additional terms are statistically significant. For example, if we fit a second-order moving average model to our data, we obtain the result shown in Table 5.2. It can be seen that the additional term (MA 2) has a p-value of 0.944. This indicates that the chances of obtaining an estimated coefficient of 0.0105, or more, are very high, if the true value of the coefficient is zero. We therefore assume that the coefficient is zero and that the additional term would add nothing to the predictive power of our original model.

5.7.3 Check 3: Are the Residuals of the Model White Noise?

If our model has extracted all of the predictive power out of the sales history, all that should remain is random variation or white noise. There should therefore be no autocorrelations in the residuals of our model's fitted values. If there were, then we could use these to improve on the predictive power of the model. For example, if there was a positive autocorrelation between successive errors, we would know that a large positive error this week tends to be followed by a large positive error next week, so a forecast that is too low tends to be followed by another forecast that is too low. If we have a positive error this week, we could then use this information to raise next week's forecast to sales that are higher than those suggested by our model, and hence improve accuracy.

Figure 5.9 shows the ACF for the residuals of our first-order moving average model. It can be seen that all of the autocorrelations

Table 5.2 Overfitting a Model

Term	Coefficient	Standard Error	t-Statistic	p-Value
Constant	25.0202	0.3945	63.42	0.000
MA1	−0.5205	0.1472	−3.54	0.001
MA2	0.0105	0.1481	0.07	0.944

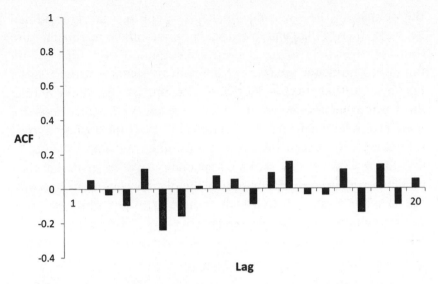

Figure 5.9 Autocorrelations of residuals

are very close to zero – any deviations from zero are probably just due to chance. The Ljung-Box statistic, often reported by software products, offers a more formal way of assessing whether the residuals are white noise. It tests whether the group of autocorrelations across the different lags are zero. If its p-value is greater than 0.05, then it indicates that the residuals probably are white noise. If it is below 0.05, then it suggests that there are still some autocorrelations in the residuals, so the model needs to be looked at again. In our case, the Ljung-Box statistic has a p-value (measured over 24 lags) of 0.398, which is consistent with the residuals being white noise.

5.7.4   Check 4: Are the Residuals Normally Distributed?

The p-values we used to test the statistical significance of the coefficients of our model, and the p-value for the Ljung-Box statistic, are based on the assumption that the sizes of the residuals are distributed according to the bell-shaped normal distribution (see Chapter 2). Figure 5.10a shows a histogram of the residuals for our model. They don't conform exactly to the bell-shaped normal distribution, but an exact match would not be expected in practice. We can do a further check by getting the computer to produce a normal probability plot, as shown in Figure 5.10b. If the distribution is exactly normal, the points will lie on a diagonal line. Because our residuals fall between the two diagonal tolerance lines, we can be reasonably sure they approximately follow a normal distribution. Note that not all forecasting software products enable you to produce the graphs in Figure 5.10a and 5.10b – they automatically assume that a normal distribution applies. However, fortunately the significance tests are quite robust to departures from normality. We should only be concerned if we have a highly skewed distribution or outliers – that is, individual residuals that are so exceptionally large or small that they lie a long way from the main body of the distribution. If this happens, one possible solution is to ask the computer to perform a Box-Cox transformation, which we discuss later.

5.8   MODELS OF NONSTATIONARY TIME SERIES: DIFFERENCING

When a series is nonstationary in the mean, the Box-Jenkins method offers a simple solution – you simply model the differences between sales in successive periods – or, if necessary, the differences of the differences. For example, if a sales history has an underlying upward linear trend, the underlying levels in successive periods might be: 10, 14, 18, 22, 26, 30 units, and so on. If we take the differences, we get +4, +4, +4, +4, and +4. It can be seen that the differences have a stationary mean of 4 units.

If we have a nonlinear trend, the underlying levels might be 4, 9, 16, 25, and 36 units. Taking differences leads to: +5, +7, +9, +11 units, and so on. Clearly, these so-called first differences are not stationary, but if we take the differences of these (second differences), we get +2, +2, +2, which is a stationary series. We can, of course, check whether the differenced series is stationary using the methods we met earlier.

Of course, most real-life sales histories will not have these constant differences. For example, the latest difference in sales might be related to the difference between the previous two periods. This would mean the first differences could be modeled by a first-order autoregressive model, such as:

Sales this week – Sales last week = 20

+ 0.6 (Sales last week – Sales two weeks ago) + Noise

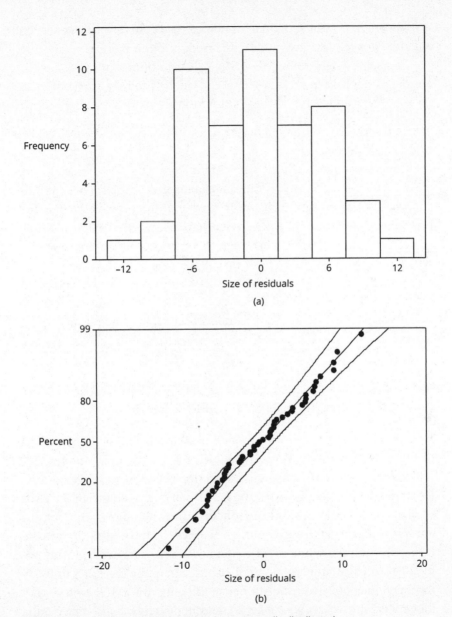

(a)

(b)

Figure 5.10 Assessing whether residuals are normally distributed

Alternatively, they might be modeled by a first-order moving average model, such as:

$$\text{Sales this week} - \text{Sales last week} = 20$$
$$+ 0.6 \text{ (Noise in previous period)} + \text{Noise}$$

where the noise is estimated by the error in forecasting the difference, not the sales themselves.

Once we have modeled the differences, we can forecast future differences and then convert these into a forecast of sales. For example, suppose we are using the above first-order autoregressive model, and this week's sales were 10 units lower than last week's. We would then forecast that the difference between this week's sales and next week's will be: $20 + 0.6(-10) = 14$ units. If we sold 200 units this week, our forecast for next week will be 214 units. Of course, computer software will carry out these sort of calculations automatically – our objective here is simply to understand what is going on "under the hood."

5.9 SHOULD YOU INCLUDE A CONSTANT IN YOUR MODEL OF A NONSTATIONARY TIME SERIES?

Note that both of the previous models have a constant of 20. The effect of this will be that, when we make a forecast using these models, we will start by assuming that the difference between next week's and this week's sales will be +20 units. We will then use the other parts of the model to add or subtract from this. It can be shown that for our autoregressive model, we would, on average, be forecasting an upward trend of 50 units, while for the moving average model, typically we would forecast an upward trend of 20 units. In many cases, it is unlikely that such increases will be sustained in the long run, and therefore, any longer-term forecasts we make using our models may be inaccurate. Because of this, the default position in some software products is not to have a constant when a series has been differenced. If you want to have a constant, you therefore have to specifically request this (usually by ticking a box), but you should only do this if you believe that future sales will continue to follow the same upward or downward trend as in the past.

5.10 WHAT IF A SERIES IS NONSTATIONARY IN THE VARIANCE?

Figure 5.2 earlier in the chapter showed a series that was nonstationary in the variance – the underlying variability of the series was changing as time progressed. When this happens, we should not fit a model to the raw sales figures, as this will reduce the efficiency with which the computer estimates the parameters of our model. This may lead to large errors in these estimates. To try to avoid this, we need to transform the sales figure in the hope that the resulting figures will be stable in their variability over time. If this works, after forecasting the transformed data we can, of course, reverse the transformation later to get a forecast in terms of actual sales.

Many software packages use the Box-Cox power transformation. This is designed to transform the data so it has a normal distribution and a constant variance. It has the form:

$$\text{Transformed sales} = \frac{(\text{Original sales})^\lambda - 1}{\lambda}$$

where λ is any number other than 0. If it equals 0, then the logarithm of sales is used instead.

For example, if we have sales of 20 units and set $\lambda = 0.5$, then the transformed sales will be:

$$[(20)^{0.5} - 1]/0.5 = 6.94$$

If you decide to use the Box-Cox transformation, the computer will automatically attempt to determine the best value of λ for the set of data, and it will automatically reverse the transformation when the forecasts of the transformed sales need to be converted to actual sales forecasts.

5.11 ARIMA NOTATION

The Box-Jenkins models for series that are nonstationary in the mean are called ARIMA models. This stands for autoregressive integrated moving average. The term *integrated* refers to the fact that the series has been differenced to achieve stationarity. The different types of models are identified using ARIMA(p, d, q) notation where p = the number of autoregressive terms in the model, d = the amount of differencing, and q = the number of moving average terms.

For example, a simple first-order autoregressive model where there has been no differencing would be an ARIMA(1,0,0) model. Similarly, a second-order moving average model based on the first differences of a sales history would be designated as an ARIMA(0,1,2) model.

A series represented by an ARIMA(0,1,0) model is known as a random walk. If we took its first differences, we would find that they are simply white noise, so the model has no autoregressive or moving average terms since these differences are merely random. The optimum forecast for sales that follow a random walk is a naïve, or no change, forecast.

5.12   SEASONAL ARIMA MODELS

Box-Jenkins models can be extended, so they can be applied to sales histories with seasonal patterns. If we have a monthly seasonal pattern, for example, we might expect sales 12 months apart to be correlated – that is, we would have an autocorrelation at a lag of 12 months. For example, we might find the following model fits our sales history:

Sales in a given month = 24 + 0.53 Sales 12 months earlier + Noise

This would be a seasonal autoregressive model of order 1 and period 12. If a series is stationary, and this type of model is appropriate, theoretically it would have an ACF and PACF with patterns like those shown in Figure 5.11. It can be seen that these are the same as those for the first-order autoregressive model that we met earlier except that the autocorrelations appear every 12 periods. They show a geometric decline in the ACF, but the PACF shows a single spike at a lag of 12 months. Of course, for quarterly data the autocorrelations and partial autocorrelations would appear at lags of 4, 8, 12, and so on.

Similarly, we might find that monthly sales are correlated with errors in the forecasts that were made for the same month, one year earlier. A typical model would be:

Sales in a given month = 130 + 0.47 Noise 12 months earlier + Noise

This would be a seasonal moving average model of order 1 and period 12. As with the nonseasonal models that we met earlier, its ACF and PACF patterns would be the reverse of those in Figure 5.11, with the single spike occurring in the ACF and the geometric decline in the PACF.

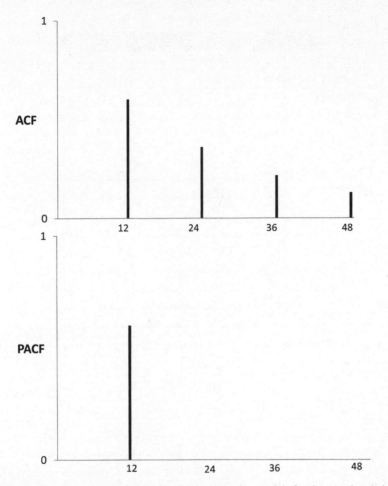

Figure 5.11 ACF and PACF for seasonal autoregressive model of order 1 and period 12

If, for monthly data, we only look at the ACF at lags 12, 24, 36, and 48 and find that these die down extremely slowly, then this suggests that the seasonal pattern is not stationary. To remedy this, we can apply seasonal differencing to the series. For monthly data, this would mean taking the difference between sales 12 months apart. For example, if we have a sales history for the last two years like that shown in Table 5.3, then the seasonal differences lead to a shorter series that starts with the difference between sales in January of Year 2 and January of Year 1. If these differences are still not stationary, we can apply second seasonal differences.

Table 5.3 Seasonal Differencing

		Sales (Units)	Seasonal Differences
Year 1	Jan	20	
	Feb	22	
	Mar	24	
	Apr	27	
	May	29	
	Jun	31	
	Jul	34	
	Aug	27	
	Sep	26	
	Oct	24	
	Nov	22	
	Dec	19	
Year 2	Jan	23	3
	Feb	26	4
	Mar	27	3
	Apr	31	4
	May	36	7
	Jun	33	2
	Jul	37	3
	Aug	28	1
	Sep	26	0
	Oct	23	−1
	Nov	25	3
	Dec	20	1

Of course, sales in each period might not only be correlated with what happened a year ago. As we saw with the nonseasonal models, they could also be correlated with what happened in much closer periods, such as the previous period. This leads to the need for models that combine the features of the nonseasonal models, which we met earlier, with those of the seasonal models. These models are known as multiplicative seasonal models (not to be confused with the multiplicative seasonal pattern that we met in Chapter 2) and are represented by the notation:

$$\text{ARIMA}(p, d, q) \times (P, D, Q)_m$$

BOX-JENKINS ARIMA MODELS ◀ 101

The bracketed small case letters refer to the nonseasonal part of the model and have the same meanings, as before, so p = the number of nonseasonal autoregressive terms, d = the amount of nonseasonal differencing, and q = the number of nonseasonal moving average terms.

The bracketed large-case letters refer, analogously, to the seasonal part of the model, so P = the number of seasonal autoregressive terms, D = the amount of seasonal differencing, and Q = the number of seasonal moving average terms. The letter m = the number of periods per year, so it will be 4 for quarterly sales or 12 for monthly sales.

Thus, a model of monthly sales, where we have only had to apply nonseasonal first differencing to achieve stationarity and which has one nonseasonal autoregressive term and one seasonal moving average term, would be an ARIMA$(1,1,0) \times (0,0,1)_{12}$ model. A commonly applied model is the ARIMA$(0,1,1) \times (0,1,1)_{12}$ model. A series represented by this model requires both nonseasonal first differencing and then seasonal first differencing to achieve stationarity. The resulting differenced series is then modeled by one nonseasonal moving average term and one seasonal moving average term. The equations for these models can be quite long and complicated to write out, so special notation (beyond the scope of this text) is required to make them concise. However, our main task is to assess the suitability of the models for our sales forecasts and to evaluate the accuracy of their forecasts. We can leave these equations and their associated algorithms to the computer.

5.13   EXAMPLE OF FITTING A SEASONAL ARIMA MODEL

Figure 5.12 shows the quarterly sales of a railroad company, measured in terms of millions of tons of freight carried over a $16\frac{1}{2}$-year period – that's 66 observations (the data are real but the source has been disguised). The series appears to be nonstationary, and the ACF shown in Figure 5.13 is consistent with this, as it dies down very slowly.

After first differencing the series, we obtain the ACF and PACF in Figure 5.14. This suggests that we have achieved stationarity. The autocorrelations at nonseasonal lags (e.g., lags 1, 2, and 3) die out quickly, while the autocorrelations at the seasonal lags (4, 8, and 12) also decline fairly quickly, so it looks as if we don't also need seasonal differencing.

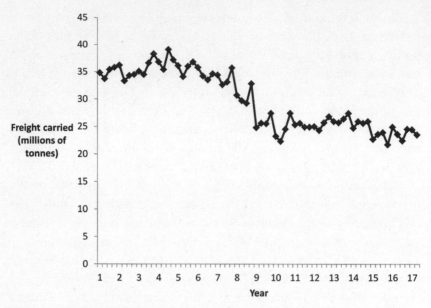

Figure 5.12 Freight carried by railroad company per quarter

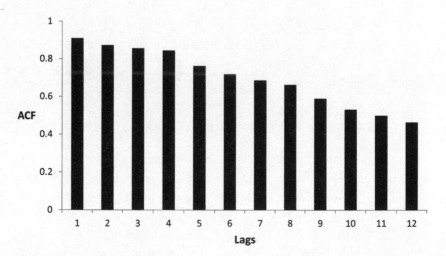

Figure 5.13 ACF for railroad data

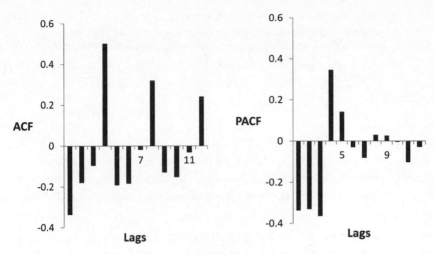

Figure 5.14 ACF and PACF after first differencing

The challenge now is to identify a tentative model, and, if we are not using an automated system, a great deal of subjective judgment is needed here. For example, we could interpret the first three lags in the ACF as being a single spike at lag 1, with the subsequent smaller spikes simply being chance autocorrelations, or we could judge that these three bars show a geometric decline in the autocorrelations. Similarly, the first three lags in the PACF could represent a geometric decline in the ACFs that has been distorted by chance factors in our sample of observations, or they could be seen as three spikes. Tentatively, we will make the initial assumptions in each case – we'll read the ACF as a single spike at lag 1 and the PACF as showing geometric decline that has been distorted. This suggests a moving average term for the nonseasonal part of our model, so, tentatively, so far we have an ARIMA$(0,1,1) \times (?, 0, ?)_4$ model.

The seasonal part of our model looks less ambiguous. In the ACF the autocorrelations show a geometric decline over lags 4, 8, and 12, and the PACF shows a single spike at lag 4 with virtually zero correlations at lags 8 and 12. This clearly suggests an autoregressive term for the seasonal part of our model, so we will now test out the fit of an ARIMA$(0,1,1) \times (1,0,0)_4$ model. We will choose not to have a constant for the reasons stared earlier. The results are shown in Table 5.4.

Table 5.4   Results for the Tentative Seasonal Model

Term	Coefficient	Standard Error	t-Statistic	p-Value
MA 1	−0.4767	0.1093	−4.79	0.000
Seasonal AR1	−0.5236	0.1112	−4.29	0.000

It's now time to carry out the diagnostic tests on our model. Table 5.4 shows that both terms in our model are highly statistically significant, as shown by their *p*-values of 0.000. For brevity, we will omit details of the remaining checks, but overfitting showed that when extra terms were added to the model, they were not statistically significant. The Ljung-Box statistic indicated that we could assume that the residuals of the model were white noise and also that these residuals appeared to be approximately normally distributed.

However, recall that when we looked at the ACF and PACF, we had difficulties in deciding whether the nonseasonal element in our model should be autoregressive or a moving average. To check this out, we could fit an ARIMA$(1,0,0) \times (1,0,0)_4$ model to the series. If we do this, it also passes all the diagnostic tests—so which should we choose? Our first model has a BIC of 1.64 and the competing model a BIC of 1.68 (see Chapter 3). It's very close, but generally models with the smaller BIC are chosen, so we will stick with our first model. However, remember that we are only comparing the fit of the models to past data here. The next step would be to compare their accuracy on a hold-out sample.

5.14   WRAP-UP

1. Box-Jenkins models exploit autocorrelations in sales histories to produce their forecasts. They therefore require that the auto-correlation remains fairly stable over time. If they do not, the exponential smoothing methods we met in the last chapter may lead to more accurate forecasts.

2. It can be shown that certain Box-Jenkins models are equivalent to particular exponential smoothing methods so the two approaches overlap, but they also offer distinct capabilities.

For example, none of the exponential smoothing methods are designed to be used for stationary time series. Even simple exponential smoothing assumes that the mean of the series (i.e., the underlying level) is subject to change over time. Similarly, some exponential smoothing methods cannot be replicated by Box-Jenkins models.

3. Some software packages have facilities for automatically identifying and fitting the most appropriate Box-Jenkins model. If these facilities are not available, identifying which model to use requires experience, skill, and judgment, as the ACFs and PACFs rarely conform exactly to the theoretical patterns associated with each model. Nevertheless, a formal set of diagnostic tests is available to signal when a model is inappropriate.

4. Care should be taken before including a constant in a model that has involved differencing, as this will imply that there is a global trend that will persist in the future. This may lead to inaccuracies in forecasts with longer lead times.

5. Seasonal Box-Jenkins models can be complex and difficult to interpret.

6. As with exponential smoothing, the Box-Jenkins models we've discussed are univariate and hence take no direct account of factors like advertising expenditure or price that might be having an effect on sales. In the next chapter, we will meet methods that are designed to take these factors into account.

5.15   SUMMARY OF KEY TERMS

Stationarity.	A condition where a sales history has the same structure, including the same underlying mean and degree of variation, over time.
Autocorrelation.	The degree of association between sales a given number of periods apart.
Partial autocorrelation.	The autocorrelation between sales separated by a given number of periods with the effect of sales in the intervening periods removed.

Autoregressive model.	A forecasting model where sales in a given period are associated with the level of sales that occurred in one or more earlier periods.
Moving average model.	A forecasting model where sales in a given period are associated with the level of noise that occurred in one or more earlier periods.
Mixed model	A forecasting model that includes both autoregressive and moving average terms.
Differencing.	First differencing is the process of subtracting sales in the previous period from each sales figure with the aim of achieving a series that is stationary in the mean. In second differencing, the differences of the differences are calculated. In seasonal differencing, sales that occurred at the same time in the previous year are subtracted from each sales figure.
Box-Cox transformation.	A transformation of sales figures that is designed to produce a series where the noise is normally distributed and has the same degree of variability in all periods.
ARMA model.	An autoregressive, moving average, or mixed model that is fitted to a series that has not required any differencing.
ARIMA model.	An autoregressive, moving average, or mixed model where differencing was required to make the series stationary before fitting the model.
Seasonal autoregressive model.	A forecasting model where sales in a given period are associated with the level of sales that occurred at the same time of year in one or more earlier years.
Seasonal moving average model.	A forecasting model where sales in a given period are associated with the level of noise that occurred at the same time of year in one or more earlier years.

ARIMA(p,d,q) ×
(P,D,Q)m.

The notation to represent a multiplicative model that has both nonseasonal and seasonal components where there are m periods in a year: p = the number of nonseasonal autoregressive terms, d = the degree of nonseasonal differencing, q = the number of nonseasonal moving average terms, P = the number of seasonal autoregressive terms, D = the degree of seasonal differencing, and Q = the number of seasonal moving average terms.

CHAPTER **6**

Regression
Models

6.1 INTRODUCTION

In the previous two chapters, we looked at univariate, or time series, forecasting methods that only used data from the sales history to produce their forecasts. These methods therefore don't make use of information on factors that might be influencing or driving sales, such as expenditure on marketing activities, pricing, or the weather. By modeling the effect of these factors, we might obtain more accurate forecasts. But this is not guaranteed; the simpler univariate methods often do better.

In this chapter, we will look at how to use your software to create models that attempt to explain variations in sales by measuring the influence of potential drivers. If you have information on the future values of these drivers, you can then use the models to produce forecasts. The models we will look at are called *regression models*. The process of obtaining these models is underpinned by a number of technical assumptions that you will find in the appendix to the chapter. We start by looking at the simplest form of regression (so-called bivariate regression) where only one factor is used to predict sales. Towards the end of the chapter we will compare the advantages and disadvantages of univariate methods and regression.

6.2 BIVARIATE REGRESSION

Consider the following example. A supermarket suspects that sales of 10.5-ounce cans of chunky chicken soup are related to the weather, with more soup being purchased in colder weather. It gathers data on sales of the product on 100 randomly selected days taken from the past year and, for each of these days, it also records the one-day-ahead forecast of midday temperature that was made for the supermarket's location. The scattergraph in Figure 6.1 displays the data.

The computer can now fit a line to the scatter of points using the least squares method that we met in Chapter 4. Figure 6.1 shows the line. This line is described by its equation, and in this case it is:

Number of cans sold per day = 488.5 − 4 × Temperature forecast

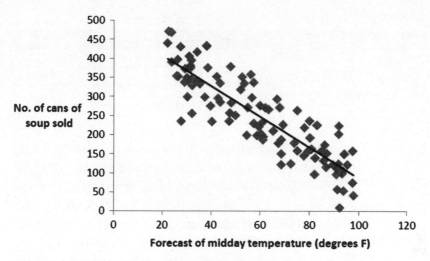

Figure 6.1   Soup sales and temperature forecast

The variable we want to predict, in our case "Number of cans sold per day," is called the *dependent* (or response) variable. The variable that drives the prediction, in our case "Temperature forecast," is called the predictor (or independent) variable. Making a forecast is simple. For example, if tomorrow's temperature is forecast to be 60 degrees Fahrenheit, then we would forecast that the supermarket will have sales of $488.5 - 4(60) = 248.5$ cans. We can't sell half a can, but the line gives a forecast of what the average sales will be on days when the midday temperature is forecast to be 60 degrees. The line also suggests that every one-degree rise in the predicted temperature will, on average, be associated with four fewer cans of soup being sold. When the temperature is zero degrees, the forecasted average number of cans sold per day is equal to the constant, that is 488.5 cans. If we extend the line to the left on the graph, this is where it will cross the vertical axis, so the constant is also referred to as the intercept.

Our scattergraph shows what happens to soup sales when the temperature forecast ranges from 22 to 98 degrees Fahrenheit. We can see that the pattern is linear across this range. A forecast made when the temperature is inside this range is an interpolation.

Table 6.1 Typical Computer Output for Bivariate Regression

Predictor	Coefficient	Standard Error	t-Statistic	p-Value
Constant	488.52	14.20	34.4	0.000
Temp forecast degrees F	−4.03	0.22	−18.2	0.000
S = 52.074	R-squared = 0.771	Adjusted R-squared	= 0.769	

If we need to make a forecast for a temperature outside this range (e.g., when the temperature is 10 degrees), we need to extend the line beyond the scatter of points. This is an extrapolation and is less reliable than interpolation because we have no data to tell us what happens to the relationship between soup sales and temperate forecasts beyond the observed range.

One concern is that the apparent relationship between the temperature forecasts and sales that we see in Figure 6.1 might simply be a result of chance. In reality, the two variables might be unrelated, but, by chance, the 100 days we sampled just happened to give the impression of a relationship. If we'd sampled another 100 days, then this impression might have disappeared. Imagine throwing 100 darts randomly at a square noticeboard – there's a possibility that by chance they'll all cluster around a straight line like the points in Figure 6.1. To allow us to test this possibility, forecasting software produces output like that shown in Table 6.1.

The table has the same structure as those we met in the last chapter when fitting ARIMA models. As before, the key numbers are the p-values. The p-value for the constant tells us the probability of estimating a value of 488.52 or more from our sample data if the true value of the constant is zero. It shows this is virtually impossible: The computer has rounded the very small probability to 0.000. We therefore conclude that the constant is not zero. This is not surprising, given the estimated value of the constant: 488.52 is a long way from zero. As in the last chapter, conventionally, we reject the hypothesis of a coefficient being zero when the p-value is below 0.05.

If, in reality, the temperature forecast has no relationship with soup sales, then its coefficient would be zero – an increase or decrease in temperature would see no change in average sales. The p-value tells us the probability of estimating a value of −4.03 or lower from our sample when the true value of the coefficient is zero. Again, the *p*-value of 0.000 tells us that this is almost impossible. Our estimate of –4.03 is simply too far from zero for zero to be a credible value. We therefore conclude the coefficient is not zero and that the association between the two variables has not arisen by chance.

As in earlier chapters, the *R*-squared value of 0.771 in Table 6.1 is a measure of how well our regression line fits the data in the scattergraph – a value of 1 being a perfect fit. The adjusted *R*-squared value serves the same purpose as it did in Chapter 4. It penalizes models for the number of predictor variables they contain (our simple model only has one) and so would enable the fit of this model to be compared with more complex models.

Finally, the S in Table 6.1 is called the standard error of the regression. It is very similar to the root mean squared error and measures how close (in terms of their vertical distance) the points on the scattergraph are to the line of best fit. It can therefore be used as an additional measure of the line's goodness of fit. Roughly speaking, it tells us that, on average, the points are 52.074 cans away from the line.

6.2.1 Should You Drop the Constant?

Our results show that it's safe to assume that the constant in our model is not zero. But suppose the *p*-value for the constant had been greater than 0.05, suggesting that a value of zero is plausible. Alternatively, suppose that we have a situation where the dependent variable must be zero if the predictor variable has this value. For example, if we have no customers in a month, we would have no sales so a "true" model might be:

No. of units sold = $3.4 \times$ Number of customers

Including a constant in this model would seem to make no sense. Most software products allow you to fit a regression model without a constant. This is also called *regression through the origin* because you are forcing the line to go through the point where both variables have a value of zero on the graph.

Should you use regression through the origin? This is a surprisingly controversial question. Many people caution against it. It can lead to curious values for R-squared, including even negative values. For this reason, some packages will not display R-squared when the constant has been dropped. When they do display the value, different software products can give different results. All of this means that assessing the fit of the model and comparing it with the fit of a model that does include a constant can be problematical.

In addition, by forcing the line to go through the origin you are changing the coefficient of the predictor variable – making the line on the graph more or less steep. This means that you may be biasing the estimate of the predictor variable's effect. For example, while a model that includes a constant might suggest that each additional $1 of advertising yields $1.8 of extra sales, a regression through the origin might estimate that each extra dollar yields $2.5 of extra sales.

At the end of the day, whether or not you drop the constant is a judgment call. But it is best only to consider doing this when: (1) The constant has a p-value of more than 0.05; (2) the regression through the origin has a smaller value for the standard error of regression, S; and (3) you have good reason to think that the constant should be zero.

6.2.2 Spurious Regression

Sometimes, when we look at different variables over time we find that, by coincidence, they have both increased or decreased together. In Chapter 2, we referred to the case where the population of Britain and the percentage of American households with a computer had both increased over the same years. It would clearly be nonsensical to infer that the two are related. Spurious regression can occur when we regress a variable that is nonstationary in the mean on to other variables that are nonstationary (see Chapter 5 for an explanation of stationarity). If we do this, the computer might mislead us into thinking that the variables are related – particularly as it might report a very high R-squared value. As with Box-Jenkins models, the solution is to difference the variables to make them stationary before applying regression analysis. For example, we may be considering forecasting using a regression model that links our weekly sales to the number of tweets that featured our product in the previous week. However, we find that both these variables have increased over time and so are nonstationary. We therefore take the difference between both variables, and a typical model might look like this:

Sales this week − Sales last week = 20 + 1.6

× (No. of tweets featuring product last week

− No. of tweets featuring product 2 weeks ago) + Noise

The computer output for this model would then indicate to us whether the relationship between the differences in sales and differences in the number of tweets featuring the product is likely to be useful in forecasting sales.

6.3 MULTIPLE REGRESSION

Sometimes we can make more accurate forecasts by linking sales to more than one predictor variable. For example, our sales might be dependent on our advertising expenditure, the unit price we charge, the time of year, the weather, and a host of other factors. If we can obtain data on these variables, then we can use multiple regression to estimate how they are related to sales. For example, a multiple regression model might look like the one below:

Weekly Sales = 24520 + 3.5 × Advertising expenditure − 12.4

× Price + 0.1 × No. of mentions on Twitter in previous week + Noise

In a week where we spend $1,000 on advertising, charge a price of $5 per unit, and where the product was mentioned on Twitter 320 times in the previous week, the model would forecast sales of:

$$24,520 + 3.5 \times 1000 − 12.4 \times 5 + 0.1 \times 320 = 27,990 \text{ units.}$$

6.3.1 Interpreting Computer Output for Multiple Regression

Table 6.2 shows the monthly sales of a product for 24 months. Also shown are the amounts spent in each month on television advertising for the product, the amount spent on newspaper advertising, and the price charged for each unit of the product.

Table 6.2 Monthly Sales of a Product and Three Potential Predictor Variables

Month	Sales (Units)	TV Ad Spend ($00)	Newspaper Ad Spend ($00)	Price ($)
1	16668	256	89	69
2	16474	212	117	65
3	16366	259	98	48
4	18571	344	61	61
5	17762	222	139	53
6	17649	229	125	51
7	16483	289	140	73
8	15326	260	82	73
9	17757	299	87	52
10	15677	175	132	53
11	19741	388	97	57
12	16691	287	135	68
13	16650	189	80	59
14	15889	286	73	72
15	15552	254	102	68
16	17983	293	66	59
17	15992	180	88	72
18	15264	299	94	63
19	15759	179	133	53
20	15744	144	138	71
21	17724	229	118	50
22	16735	184	81	66
23	18824	381	135	56
24	18097	292	90	50

Forecasting software was used to fit a multiple regression model to the data, and it produced the output in Table 6.3. There are four key sets of results to look for in the output:

1. *The regression equation.*

This indicates that more TV advertising is associated with increased sales, while higher prices are associated with reduced sales – results we would expect. However, higher newspaper advertising appears to reduce sales, which is counterintuitive. We will explain this later.

Table 6.3 Computer Output for Multiple Regression

The regression equation is
Sales = 17931 + 10.9 TV ad spend − 0.55 Newspaper ad spend − 61.8 Price

Predictor	Coefficient	Standard Error	t-Statistic	p-Value	
Constant	17931	1917	9.35	0.000	
TV ad spend	10.882	2.856	3.81	0.001	
Newspaper ad spend	−0.546	7.227	−0.08	0.941	
Price	−61.77	21.12	−2.93	0.008	
S = 845.307 R-Sq = 0.576 R-Sq(adj) = 0.512					
Analysis of Variance					
Source	DF	SS	MS	F	p-value
Regression	3	19374903	6458301	9.04	0.001
Residual error	20	14290867	714543		
Total	23	33665771			

2. *The goodness of fit of the model to the data.*

As with bivariate regression, this is indicated by S and R-squared. The R-squared value of 0.576 shows that the model is explaining 57.6% of the variation in sales across the months. Other factors, such as possibly the actions of competitors, the weather, and noise, account for the remaining variation. The adjusted R-squared penalizes this model for its relative complexity – it is using three predictor variables. This would allow us to compare its goodness of fit with that of models that are more or less complex.

3. *The p-value for the F-statistic.*

Toward the bottom of the output, in the Analysis of Variance section, you will see an F column and a p-value of 0.001 next to it. If, in reality, sales are related to none of our predictor variables, then we would have a model that looked like this (we'll call it the null model):

$$\text{Sales} = \text{Constant} + 0 \times \text{TV ad spend} + 0 \times \text{Newspaper ad spend} + 0 \times \text{Price} + \text{Noise}$$

Note that all of the predictor variables would have coefficients of zero. For example, increases or decreases in television advertising expenditure would have no effect on sales. In this case, our model would, of course, be useless for forecasting. To test whether the model in our output has arisen by chance when the true relationship is the one shown by the null model, we use the p-value for the F-statistic. Conventionally, we reject the null model when this p-value is less than 0.05. Our model has a p-value of 0.001, so we can reject the null model and assume that at least one of our predictor variables has a nonzero coefficient.

4. *The* p-*values for the predictors.*

The test involving the F-statistic is quite a weak one. It simply indicates that at least one of our predictor variables is useful, but it doesn't tell us which ones. We want our model to be as simple as possible. For example, it may cost us money to obtain data on the predictors so, if some of them are contributing nothing to forecast accuracy, then we should remove them from the model. The p-values for the predictors allow us to assess whether each predictor's true coefficient is zero. We can interpret them in the same way as for bivariate regression. For example, the probability that television advertising spend would have an estimated coefficient of 10.882 or more when the true value is zero is only 0.001 (or one in a thousand). So we assume that the true value is not zero and we keep this predictor in our model. The same is true for Price. However, the estimated coefficient of –0.55 for Newspaper advertising spend is close to zero. The relevant p-value tells us that there is a 0.941 probability of estimating this value or less when the true value of the coefficient is zero. It's therefore quite plausible that newspaper advertising has no effect on the product's sales and we should seriously consider dropping it from our model. The apparent negative effect of newspaper advertising on sales is almost certainly reflecting a chance pattern in the data rather than a systematic relationship.

6.3.2 Refitting the Model

If we decide to eliminate a predictor variable, we need to re-estimate the model because the estimated values of the coefficients will now change at least slightly. Table 6.4 shows the computer output for the new model (for brevity the Analysis of Variance section has been omitted). We see that all of the remaining predictor variables have coefficients with p-values well below 0.05. Although R-squared has declined very slightly (from 0.576 to 0.575), the adjusted R-squared has increased (from 0.512 to 0.535) suggesting that, after taking into account model complexity, we now have a better model.

6.3.3 Multicollinearity

If some of the predictor variables are themselves highly correlated, we have an issue called *multicollinearity* (when just two are correlated we can simply use the term *collinearity*). Multicollinearity might occur, for example, where a company has regular product promotions

Table 6.4 Output for Refitted Model

The regression equation is				
Sales = 17842 + 10.9 TV ad spend − 61.5 Price				
Predictor	**Coefficient**	**Standard Error**	**t-Statistic**	**p-Value**
Constant	17842	1481	12.04	0.000
TV ad spend	10.939	2.688	4.07	0.001
Price	−61.49	20.29	−3.03	0.006
S = 825.052 R-Sq = 0.575 R-Sq(adj) = 0.535				

backed by advertising in different media. A sales forecasting model that contained four predictor variables relating to expenditure on television advertising, poster advertising, radio advertising, and newspaper advertising would be quite likely to suffer from multicollinearity because the four variables would be highly correlated. They would all be at high levels at the same time when the campaign was taking place and all at lower levels when there was no campaign. Because of the high correlations, the computer would have difficulties in disentangling the separate effects of each type of advertising. Are the high sales we usually see during promotion campaigns caused by the television advertising or the poster advertising? The regression analysis can't tell because they are always both high during campaigns. There is no data where expenditure on television advertising is high and money spent on poster advertising is low, and vice versa, so we never get to see the separate effects of the different forms of advertising.

Specifically, multicollinearity can cause three problems:

1. *It can lead to large errors in the estimates of coefficients of the prediction variables*. For example, the model in Table 6.4 estimated a coefficient of 10.9 for television advertising expenditure, suggesting that each extra $100 spent on TV advertising increase sales, on average, by 10.9 units. If the estimate had been affected by multicollinearity, the true coefficient may have been very different from this value. Indeed, there may be occasions where a negative coefficient is estimated where the true value is positive and vice versa. Computer software is likely to be unreliable when multicollinearity is high and different software products may estimate different models from the same data.

2. *If you use the model for extrapolation, the forecast will not be reliable*. That is, if you produce forecasts where the values of the predictor variables are outside the range of values we have used to estimate the model, then the forecast is likely to have a large error. To see this, suppose we have estimated the following model:

$$\text{Weekly sales} = 230 + 20 \times \text{Weekly minutes of TV advertising}$$
$$+ 16 \times \text{Weekly minutes of radio advertising}$$

However, because of collinearity, the estimated coefficient for minutes of TV advertising has a large error. Its true value is 60, not 20. Next week, for the first time, we will only advertise on television where we will buy five minutes of advertising. Our model forecasts that sales will be $230 + 20 \times 5 = 330$ units. Using the true coefficient, our forecast will be $230 + 60 \times 5 = 530$ units.

3. *The p-values for the coefficients in the model can be misleading.* They can suggest that we should drop predictor variables that are, in fact, useful predictors. This is because the *p*-values tend to be too high—that is, they tend not to fall below 0.05 when they should.

Detecting multicollinearity and ascertaining if it is a problem can be difficult. Simply looking at the correlations between the predictor variables can be helpful, but there are more insidious forms of the condition. This exists where linear combinations of some predictor variables are correlated with others. For example: TV advertising spend = 3 × Radio advertising spend + 4 Newspaper advertising spend.

So what strategy should you adopt if you suspect multicollinearity may be present in your data?

1. *Even if it exists, multicollinearity may not be a problem anyway.*

Multicollinearity is not likely to be a concern if your forecasts are interpolations and if you are not interested in knowing the individual effects of each predictor; for example, whether TV advertising is more effective than newspaper advertising.

2. *If you are still concerned, ask your software to calculate VIFs, if these are available.*

A VIF, or variance inflation factor, reflects the imprecision in the estimate of a predictor variable that is caused by multicollinearity. The computer will calculate a VIF for each predictor variable. If a predictor variable has VIF of 1, this indicates that it has no correlation with the other predictors. As a rule of thumb, a VIF greater than 4 is a warning that multicollinearity might be causing problems, while a VIF over 10 is a sign of serious multicollinearity that needs attention. For our original model the VIFs were 1.1 for both TV advertising spend and Newspaper advertising spend and 1.0 for Price, so there was no evidence that multicollinearity was a problem. The high p-value for "Newspaper ad spend" in Table 6.3 could not therefore be blamed on multicollinearity.

3. *If your software does not calculate VIFs, there are other ways of detecting multicollinearity.*

   Multicollinearity may be present if some of the following conditions apply.

   a. When you drop a variable from the model that you suspect may be collinear, the estimated coefficients of one or more of the other variables will see a large change.

   b. The p-value for the F-test is less than 0.05, but the p-values for the individual predictor variables are all greater than 0.05.

   c. A predictor variable that should be related to sales has a p-value greater than 0.05.

   d. The coefficient of a predictor variable has a sign that seems implausible. For example, the model suggests that higher advertising expenditure is associated with lower sales.

   e. The correlations between pairs of predictor values are large.

4. *You have several options if multicollinearity is present and is causing problems.*

   a. If you can, collect more data. A larger sample should improve the precision with which the coefficients of the predictor variables are estimated.

   b. Combine the predictors where this makes sense. For example, expenditure on TV advertising, radio advertising, and newspaper advertising could be combined into a single predictor variable: Total expenditure on advertising.

   c. Drop one of the collinear predictor variables from the model. This is appropriate where the variable is largely duplicating the information provided by another variable and so is virtually redundant.

More advanced strategies are also available, such as ridge regression and partial least squares, but none of these offer perfect solutions, and they may not be available in your software product.

6.3.4 Using Dummy Predictor Variables in Your Regression Model

Sometimes we can increase the accuracy of forecasts from a multiple regression model by including predictor variables that are nominal. Nominal variables are not measured by numbers. Examples include whether a customer is male or female, their sales region, the month in which they are buying the product, and the form of transport they use to get to work. We may arbitrarily assign numbers to nominal variables for convenience. For example, we might use a code of 1 for the North sales region, 2 for the South, and 3 for the West, but these numbers are merely labels. It does not make sense to say that the West region is in some way three times the North. When a computer file contains numbers like these, it's easy to make the mistake of forgetting that they are arbitrary by attempting to fit a model to the numbers. Of course, if you change the arbitrary coding (e.g., making the North 3 and the West 1), you'll get a different model. Note that nominal variables are also referred to as categorical variables.

So how can we include nominal variables in our models? The answer is relatively straightforward. We create a new variable for each category that the nominal variable can take on. For example, for gender we could have two variables, Male and Female. The variable "Male" would have a value of 1 if a person was male and 0, otherwise. Similarly, "Female" would equal 1 if a person was female and 0 if the person was male. These variables, which can only take on values of 0 or 1, are called *dummy variables*. For seasons of the year, we would have four dummy variables. For example, the variable "Winter" would only equal 1 if the data relates to that season. For months of the year we would have 12 dummy variables, and so on.

Table 6.5 shows the data we used in our earlier example, together with four new columns indicating the season in which each month occurred. The data for newspaper advertising expenditure has been

Table 6.5 Sales Data with Dummy Variables Added.

Month	Sales (units)	TV ad spend ($00)	Price ($)	Winter	Spring	Summer	Fall
1	16668	256	69	0	0	1	0
2	16474	212	65	0	1	0	0
3	16366	259	48	1	0	0	0
4	18571	344	61	1	0	0	0
5	17762	222	53	0	0	1	0
6	17649	229	51	0	1	0	0
7	16483	289	73	0	0	0	1
8	15326	260	73	1	0	0	0
9	17757	299	52	0	0	0	1
10	15677	175	53	1	0	0	0
11	19741	388	57	0	0	1	0
12	16691	287	68	0	0	0	1
13	16650	189	59	0	1	0	0
14	15889	286	72	0	0	0	1
15	15552	254	68	1	0	0	0
16	17983	293	59	0	1	0	0
17	15992	180	72	0	0	1	0
18	15264	299	63	1	0	0	0
19	15759	179	53	1	0	0	0
20	15744	144	71	0	0	1	0
21	17724	229	50	0	1	0	0
22	16735	184	66	0	0	1	0
23	18824	381	56	0	0	0	1
24	18097	292	50	0	0	0	1

removed, as we dropped that variable from our model. The table shows that the first month was a summer month and the second a spring month. We have added the dummy variables because we suspect that our sales follow a seasonal pattern. It is now tempting to fit a regression model to all six predictor variables in Table 6.5 – TV advertising spend, Price, and the four dummies. However, if we did, we would have a problem. The four dummy variables will exhibit perfect multicollinearity. For example, Winter = 1 – Spring – Summer – Fall,

Table 6.6 Computer Output for Model with Dummy Variables

The regression equation is
Sales = 17442 + 13.3 TV ad spend ($00) − 68.3 Price ($)
− 648 Winter + 665 Spring + 1032 Summer

Predictor	Coefficient	Standard Error	t-Statistic	p-Value
Constant	17442	1069	16.32	0.000
TV ad spend	13.32	1.863	7.15	0.000
Price	-68.3	13.02	-5.25	0.000
Winter	-648.2	295.9	-2.19	0.042
Spring	664.6	342.3	1.94	0.068
Summer	1031.5	320.5	3.22	0.005
S = 497.210 R-Sq = 0.868 R-Sq(adj) = 0.831				

so any one variable has a perfect linear relationship with the others. The same would be true of we used two dummy variables for gender or all 12 for months of the year. For the computer trying to estimate a model, this will be akin to dividing a number by zero and it would not be able to complete its calculations.

The solution is simple. We drop one of the dummy variables. If you have two categories, as with gender, you only use one dummy variable in your model. If you have 12 categories, as with months, you use 11 dummies, and so on. As we'll see, it doesn't matter which dummy variable you decide to drop; the model will automatically adapt to this and give you the same forecasts. In our example, we will drop the variable Fall. Table 6.6 shows the computer output for our fitted model (again, for brevity the Analysis of Variance section has been omitted).

When the variables Winter, Spring, and Summer all equal zero, we must have a Fall month. For a fall month, when we are spending $300,000 on TV advertising and setting a price of $60 for our product, the model will make the following forecasts.

$$\text{Sales} = 17{,}442 + 13.3 \times 300 - 68.3 \times 60 - 648 \times 0 + 665 \times 0 + 1032 \times 0$$

$$= 17{,}334 \text{ units}$$

If we have the same advertising expenditure and price but are forecasting a winter month, our forecast will be:

$$Sales = 17,442 + 13.3 \times 300 - 68.3 \times 60 - 648 \times 1 + 665 \times 0 + 1032 \times 0$$
$$= 16,686 \text{ units}$$

It can be seen that the Winter forecast is the same as that for the Fall except for a reduction of 648 units. Thus, the coefficients of the dummy variables in our model tell us the size of adjustment we should make to our forecasts if we are forecasting for a month in any season other than the Fall. The model estimates that, if all else remains equal, a spring month will see sales 665 units higher than a fall month, while in a summer month we can expect sales to be 1032 units higher.

Our decision to drop the variable, Fall, from our model was arbitrary. If instead we had dropped Winter, the computer would have estimated the following model.

$$Sales = 16,794 + 13.3 \text{ TV ad spend} - 68.3 \text{ Price} + 1,313 \text{ Spring}$$
$$+ 1,680 \text{ Summer} + 648 \text{ Fall}$$

For a winter month, with \$300,000 spent on TV advertising and a price for our product of \$60 (the same conditions that we had previously), the model will forecast:

$$Sales = 16,794 + 13.3 \times 300 - 68.3 \times 60 + 1,313 \times 0 + 1,680 \times 0$$
$$+ 648 \times 0 = 16686 \text{ units}$$

So we have exactly the same forecast as the one we saw earlier. It can be seen that the coefficients of the dummy variables are telling the same story. In the first model, summer's sales were expected to be 1,032 units above fall's, while winter's were expected to be 648 below. In the second model, summer's sales are expected to be 1,680 above winter's, which is the same as $1,032 + 648$ units.

Table 6.6 shows that the p-values for Winter and Summer are below 0.05, but for Spring the p-value is 0.068. This suggests that the true coefficient for Spring may be zero, which would imply that its sales tend to be the same as those of a month in the fall, if all else remains equal. So should we drop Spring from our model? The answer is no. If we were to drop Spring, our model would now be comparing sales in the remaining seasons with those in both spring and fall. This would make the model more difficult to interpret, and the coefficients for the remaining seasons would change. They might even themselves become nonsignificant with p-values above 0.05. Dummy variables should live together or die together. Only consider removing them from the model if they *all* have p-values above 0.05.

6.3.5 Outliers and Influential Observations

In Chapter 2 we saw how an unusual observation can distort the estimate of the correlation between two variables. Sometimes these observations occur because of an error in entering data, but they can also reflect freak or unusual conditions. In regression, we can distinguish between two types of unusual observation: Outliers and influential observations. It is easiest to show these in relation to bivariate regression, but they can also affect multiple regression models. Figure 6.2 shows an outlier. These occur above or below the main scatter of points, but they have little influence on the estimated model. In the example, the model fitted to all the data is: Sales = 20.9 + 4.3 × Advertising. If we fit it to data with the observation removed, it is: Sales = 18.3 + 4.3 × Advertising. The lines for both models are shown in Figure 6.2, and it's clear that the presence of the outlier has little effect.

In contrast, influential observations lie to the left or right of the main scatter. They tend to pull the line towards them and are said to have leverage. Figure 6.3 shows an influential observation. When it is included in the data set used to estimate the model, we obtain a line of best fit of Sales = 43.7+ 3.2 × Advertising. If we exclude it, the line of best fit is: Sales = 18.3 + 4.3 × Advertising. In this case the lines are clearly very different. Both lines are plotted in Figure 6.3 where the disproportionate influence of the influential observation can be clearly seen.

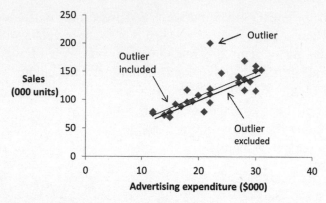

Figure 6.2   The effect of an outlier on the line of best fit

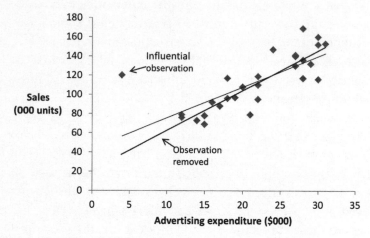

Figure 6.3   The effect of an influential observation on the line of best fit

Some software products highlight outliers and influential observations, but many do not. If they can be identified, both types of observation may merit further investigation to establish how they have occurred. If an influential observation is distorting the estimated model, it is worth considering removing it from the data. Alternatively, you could use a dummy variable to represent the special conditions that caused it to occur. For example, if the unusual figure has been caused by a strike, then you could add a variable Strike to the model, which equals 1 when a strike has taken place and 0, otherwise.

6.4   REGRESSION VERSUS UNIVARIATE METHODS

Should you use regression or the univariate methods we met in the previous two chapters to produce your sales forecasts? There are four relative advantages of regression:

1. Because they use information on potential drivers of sales, regression models may be more accurate than univariate methods in some circumstances but, as we pointed out in the introduction, this will not always be the case.

2. Regression models can produce explanations for variations in sales, which can lead to more insightful forecasting.

3. Because regression provides explanations for its forecasts, these *may* be more credible to managers than "blind" extrapolation methods like exponential smoothing.

4. Methods like simple exponential smoothing and ARIMA models are designed for short-term forecasting. For example, simple exponential smoothing forecasts for more than one period ahead form a flat line on a graph. Regression models can use information on the future values of predictor variables (e.g., the advertising budget in six months' time) to forecast a long way ahead.

However, regression also has six disadvantages:

1. Data has to be collected on the predictor variables. This may be costly and time consuming. With the univariate methods, you only need the sales history.

2. In many cases you need to forecast the future values of the predictor variables before you can forecast sales. For example, if next month's sales depend on the weather, then you'll need to forecast the weather a month ahead to produce your sales forecast. This will compound the forecast errors and is likely to reduce accuracy.

3. The regression models we have met are global models so they are not designed to adapt to change. For example, if advertising is becoming less effective, a forecasting model based on a

past relationship between sales and advertising will eventually become out-of-date. More advanced forms of regression can adapt, but these come at the cost of greater complexity.

4. All the regression models in this chapter assumed linear relationships between sales and the predictor variables. For example, each extra dollar of expenditure on advertising was assumed to bring the same increase in sales. In practice, advertising expenditure may be subject to diminishing returns as it increases. It's possible to build nonlinear relationships into regression models (e.g., by using logs) and also to incorporate interactions between predictor variables where, for example, their joint effect is greater than the sum of their individual effects, but again this leads to more complexity in the modeling process.

5. It is easier to automate the univariate methods, particularly exponential smoothing, which is important if the sales of a large number of products have to be forecast regularly. There are ways of automatically fitting a multiple regression model. These include a method called stepwise regression. However, this and similar methods suffer from a problem known as *model selection bias*, which leads to biases in the estimates of model coefficients. They are also inconsistent – different methods can lead to different models being selected.

   Applying regression is an art as much as a science, and careful judgment and expertise are usually required on whether variables should be included in the model, even if their p-values are greater than 0.05. We may wish to include such variables where we suspect that there is multicollinearity or where we have an insignificant dummy variable. Sometimes we may have a sound theoretical reason to include a variable, even though its p-value is over 0.05. Applying judgment to develop individual regression models for thousands of products is obviously impractical.

6. In some cases, the theoretical assumptions underlying regression analysis (see Appendix) may be seriously violated.

This can invalidate the *p*-values and the efficiency of the estimated model. While there are usually solutions to these problems, detecting the violations and applying the remedies can be complex and time-consuming.

6.5 DYNAMIC REGRESSION

One of the important assumptions of regression analysis is that the errors or residuals of a model are random and hence have zero auto-correlations. This means that knowing the latest error will be of no use in predicting subsequent errors. This is analogous to tossing a die. If you know that a 3 just came up, this will not help you to forecast the score on the next throw. When this assumption is violated, it means that we have not extracted all of the useful predictive information from our data. It also means that many of the results that the computer supplies will be misleading (see Appendix). We had similar concerns in Chapter 5 when we looked at Box-Jenkins models and tested to see whether the residuals were white noise.

If the residuals of the regression model are not random, one way of dealing with this is to use dynamic regression. Dynamic regression combines the type of regression model we have been discussing with a Box-Jenkins ARIMA model. The ARIMA model is used to represent the residuals or errors. For example, a typical dynamic regression model might look like this:

$$\text{Monthly demand} = 4,235 + 23 \times \text{Advertising expenditure} - 8$$
$$\times \text{Price} + \text{Error}$$

$$\text{Where: Error} = 0.8 + 0.3 \times \text{Previous error} + \text{Noise}$$

Because the error in the first equation cannot be assumed to be random, it is modeled by the second equation – in this example, a first-order autocorrelation model. If the dynamic regression model is appropriate, then the noise in this second equation will be random and hence will be white noise.

Dynamic regression models are relatively complex and, because of the number of coefficients that need to be estimated, they require a large amount of data. More details of the procedure for fitting these types of models can be found in more advanced texts, such as *Forecasting Principles and Practice* by Rob Hyndman and George Athanasopoulos.

6.6   WRAP-UP

1. Regression models attempt to provide explanations for variations in sales by modeling the relationship between sales and the factors (or predictor variables) that drive them. Once this relationship has been estimated, sales forecasts can be made as long as we know the values of the predictor variables that will apply in the period that we are forecasting.

2. Computer software will estimate the model that best fits the data and provide statistics that can be used to assess its validity. However, applying regression is both an art and a science, so judgment and expertise are needed to apply the method successfully. In particular, care needs to be taken when the predictor variables exhibit multicollinearity, which is common in practice.

3. There is no guarantee that a regression model will produce more accurate forecasts than a univariate model, despite the fact that it uses more information.

6.7   SUMMARY OF KEY TERMS

Dependent variable.	The variable to be predicted. In our case, this will usually be sales or demand.
Predictor or independent variable.	A variable that is associated with sales and can therefore be used to forecast them (e.g., advertising expenditure or price per unit).
The constant or intercept.	The forecast that would be produced by a regression model if all the predictor variables had a value of zero.
Interpolation.	A forecast made by a regression model when the predictor variables have values that fall within the range of values that were used to fit the model.

Extrapolation.	A forecast made by a regression model when the predictor variables have values that falls beyond the range of values that were used to fit the model. Extrapolation is therefore less reliable than interpolation.
R-*squared.*	A measure of how well the regression model fits the data. It has a value between 0 and 1 (or 0 and 100%) where 1 indicates a perfect fit.
Adjusted R-*squared.*	The R-squared value adjusted so that it penalizes more complex models based on the number of predictors they have.
Standard error of the regression.	Another measure of how well the regression model fits the data. Roughly speaking, it measures how close the actual observations are, on average, to the model's fitted values. Unlike R-squared, it has no upper limit.
Spurious regression.	A regression model that wrongly suggests that unrelated variables have a strong relationship. It arises when the variables in the model are represented by time series that are nonstationary.
Null model.	A regression model where all of the predictor variables have coefficients of zero, so it only consists of a constant. Effectively, it assumes that none of the predictor variables have any association with sales.
The p-*value for the* F *statistic.*	This is used to test whether the estimated regression model differs significantly from a null model. Conventionally, if the p-value is less than 0.05, we can assume that it does and therefore at least one of the predictor variables is related to sales.
The p-*values for the individual predictor variables.*	These are used to test whether the coefficient of each predictor variable differs significantly from zero. Conventionally, if the p-value is less than 0.05, we can assume that it does and therefore the predictor variable is related to sales.

Multicollinearity.	A condition where the predictor variables are correlated or where linear combinations of the predictor variables are correlated.
Dummy predictor variable.	Predictor variables that take on a value of either 0 or 1, depending on whether a particular condition (e.g., a particular sales region or a particular month) applies to an observation.
Outlier.	An observation where the dependent variable (e.g., sales) has a value that is much higher or lower than the mass of other observations, despite the predictor variables having values that fall within the typical range.
Influential observation.	An observation where both the dependent variable and the predictor variables take on extreme values. Because such observations can distort the estimated model, they are said to be influential.
Dynamic regression.	A method that is used when the residuals of a regression model are not random so they are autocorrelated. An ARMA or ARIMA model is used to model these residuals.

6.8 APPENDIX: ASSUMPTIONS OF REGRESSION ANALYSIS

1. The form of the model is correct. This would be violated where a linear model is being used when the true relationship between sales and a predictor variable is nonlinear.

2. For a given value of the predictor variable, the errors, or residuals, associated with the regression line's prediction follow the bell-shaped normal distribution. We made the same assumption when fitting the Box-Jenkins ARIMA models in the last chapter. Only serious violations of this assumption are a concern.

3. For every value of the predictor variable, the variation of the possible forecast errors is the same. This is known as homoscedasticity. For example, this assumption would be

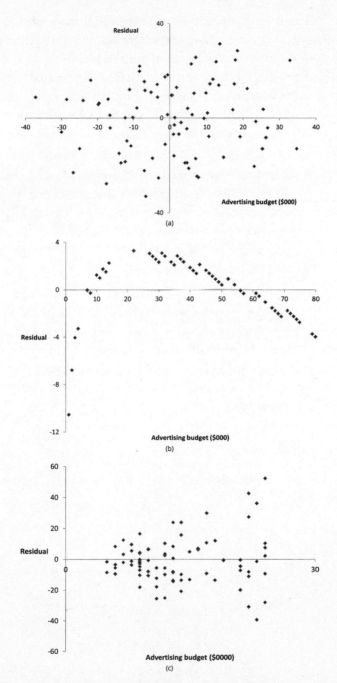

Figure 6.4 Using residual plots to detect violations of assumptions

violated if the chances of a large error in a sales forecast increased as advertising expenditures got bigger – ideally, we should expect the same risk of large errors at any level of advertising. When the assumption is violated, we have a condition called heteroscedasticity and, when it occurs, it means that we cannot trust the p-values for the F-test or for the individual coefficients.

4. The errors, or residuals, of the model are independent of each other. For example, once we know the error of one forecast, we can't use it to predict the error that will be associated with other forecasts. When this assumption is violated, we can't trust the value of R-squared or the p-values for the F-test or the individual coefficients. In addition, our estimates of the model's coefficients may be unstable.

Some software products allow you to plot the residuals against the predictor variables to check whether the assumptions are violated. Figure 6.4a shows an example where there is no evidence of assumptions being violated. Figure 6.4b suggests that a linear model has been fitted when the relationship is nonlinear. Figure 6.4c suggests that we have the problem of heteroscedacity – the scatter of the residuals gets wider as the advertising budget increases.

6.9 REFERENCE

Hyndman, R. J., and Athanasopoulos, G. (2013). Forecasting principles and practice. *OTexts*.

CHAPTER 7

Inventory Control, Aggregation, and Hierarchies

7.1 INTRODUCTION

In many organizations, forecasts guide decisions on how much safety, or buffer, stock to hold to reduce the probability of stock-outs to an acceptable level. The point forecasts we have focused on in the preceding chapters are not sufficient to provide this guidance – we also need to know how much uncertainty surrounds the point forecasts. For example, if we have a point forecast for next month's sales of 200 units, the actual sales might turn out to be anywhere between 80 and 320 units, so we need to take this into account when deciding on our inventory levels. In this chapter, we will look at how computer software estimates uncertainty and how this can be used in inventory planning.

It is important to distinguish between a demand forecast and an inventory decision. A demand forecast is an estimate of what is likely to happen to sales in a future period. An inventory decision is a manager's choice of how much stock should be held in light of the forecast. For example, the forecast might indicate that the most likely level of sales next month is 300 units. However, to cope with the possibility of higher demand than this, we may decide to have 360 units in stock at the start of the month. If we call the latter figure a forecast, then other managers might mistakenly think that 360 units is the most likely level of sales and make their decisions on this basis. In addition, our forecast accuracy is likely to look awful if we compare these inventory decisions to the actual sales, rather than the true forecasts.

We can often get more reliable forecasts to guide our inventory decisions if the individual periods in our sales histories are longer (e.g., if they are records of weekly rather than daily sales or monthly sales rather than weekly). Later in the chapter we will look at how the process of converting high-frequency records (e.g., daily sales) to those with a lower frequency (e.g., weekly sales) can be implemented. The process is called temporal aggregation.

Finally, we will look at another form of aggregation. Sales figures are often recorded at different levels so they form hierarchies. For example, we can have records of a company's total sales, of its sales by product type, and of its sales of individual products. However, if we aggregate all the sales forecasts for individual products, we will rarely arrive at the same figure as we would if we made a direct forecast of total sales. We will therefore explore a number of methods available in forecasting packages that are designed to overcome this problem by reconciling forecasts at different levels in a hierarchy.

7.2 IDENTIFYING REORDER LEVELS AND SAFETY STOCKS

When deciding on inventory levels, managers have to balance two costs – holding and stock-out costs. The cost of holding inventory includes storage and insurance costs and the financial returns that could have been earned had money been invested elsewhere rather than in inventory. There is also a risk that stock will deteriorate and, hence, lose its value during storage, or that it will become obsolete before it is sold.

A stock-out occurs when there is demand for a product that we cannot meet. Stock-out costs can be more difficult to measure, but they include loss of profit resulting from demand that cannot be fulfilled, the cost of emergency production runs, and the losses arising from damaged customer goodwill. It usually makes no sense to have a policy of never having a stock-out – unless, for example, the product is a life-saving drug – because the holding costs would be unduly expensive. As a result, organizations often aim to meet demand on, say, 95% of occasions so they would only disappoint customers in one out of every twenty periods on average.

In a continuous review inventory system, we constantly monitor stock levels. We allow these to be depleted until they reach a level where it is necessary to place an order for replenishments. This is called the reorder level (or reorder point). Usually the order will take some time to be delivered. The time between placing the order and receiving the new supplies is called the lead time. We need to set the reorder level to ensure that we still have sufficient stocks to keep us going while we await the delivery – albeit allowing for a predetermined risk of a stock-out. To achieve this, ideally we need to know the probabilities of different levels of demand in the lead time.

It is common to assume that demand follows the bell-shaped normal distribution like the one displayed in Figure 7.1. Here the expected (or mean) level of demand in the lead time is 2,200 units, but it can

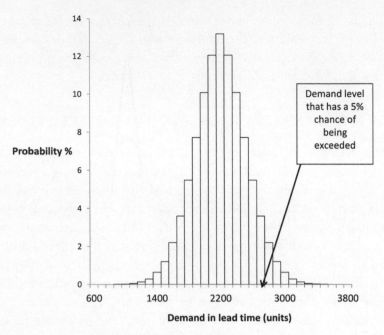

Figure 7.1 Normal probability distribution of demand

be seen that demand can vary to below 1,400 and above 3,000 units. The diagram suggests that a demand of about 2,800 units is exceeded only 5% of the time, so if we want to achieve that customer service level, we should have 2,800 units in stock at the start of the lead time. The safety stock is the difference between the expected level of demand during the lead time (2,200 units) and the amount of stock we decide to hold at the start of the lead time (i.e., the reorder level) to allow only a 5% chance of a stock-out (2,800 units). In this case, it is therefore 600 units.

To obtain a probability distribution like that in Figure 7.1, we need to estimate two things: The expected level of demand for the lead time and the possible variation around this resulting from noise. The variation is measured by the standard deviation (SD). Figure 7.2 shows probability distributions of demand in the period-to-be-forecast for different standard deviations. Here, we have replaced the histogram display with smooth curves (for technical reasons, we now label the vertical axis probability density). The diagram shows that the distribution has a greater spread when the standard deviation is larger.

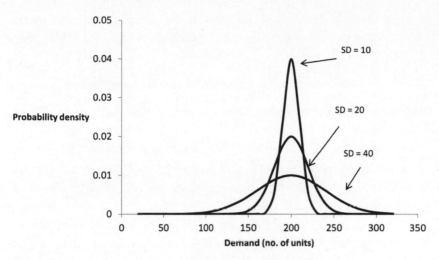

Figure 7.2 Normal distributions with different standard deviations

Once we know the expected demand and the standard deviation for the lead time, we can determine the amount of stock we need to meet a given customer service level by using the following formula:

Reorder level

= Expected demand in lead time + Z × Standard deviation.

Here Z depends on the service level required and can obtained from published tables. Table 7.1 shows some typical values.

Table 7.1 Z values for Different Customer Service Levels

Probability of Stock-Out	Z
0.5%	2.58
1.0%	2.33
2.0%	2.05
2.5%	1.96
4.0%	1.75
5.0%	1.65
10.0%	1.28
20.0%	0.84

For example, if the expected demand for a lead time is 450 units, the standard deviation is 50 units, and we want to allow a 2% chance of a stock-out, then:

$$\text{Reorder level} = 450 + 2.05 \times 50 = 553 \text{ units}$$

which indicates that we should be carrying $553 - 450 = 103$ units of safety stock.

It can be seen that the standard deviation reflects the amount of uncertainty we have about demand during the lead time, and the larger it is, the greater the amount of safety stock we will need to achieve a given customer service level.

The previous examples assumed that we constantly monitor our stock levels and place a new order as soon as stocks are depleted to the reorder level. However, in some inventory systems, known as period review systems, stock levels are only reviewed periodically at particular times (e.g., once a month). If the review suggests that replenishments are needed, an order is placed. In this system, we need to ensure that the size of our order is sufficient to brings stocks up to a level that will meet demand, not just for the review period, but also for the subsequent lead time. For example, suppose the lead time is two weeks and our review period is four weeks. If we are ordering new supplies today, we won't be placing another order for another four weeks, and that order will take two further weeks to arrive. We therefore need to cover demand for the next $4 + 2 = 6$ weeks. Hence, we need a probability distribution of demand for the period covered by the review interval plus the lead time. For conciseness, in the discussion that follows we will only refer to demand in the lead time, but if you are operating a periodic review system, you should substitute the term *review period plus lead time* where "lead time" appears.

7.3 ESTIMATING THE PROBABILITY DISTRIBUTION OF DEMAND

How can forecasting software be used to estimate the probability distribution of future demand? The expected demand in the lead time is simply equal to the point forecast. However, estimating the standard deviation is more challenging, and a number of methods are used.

The simplest approach is to calculate the root mean square error (RMSE) of past forecasts (see Chapter 3) and use the square root of this as the estimate of the standard deviation. For example, if the last 50 forecasts we made had an MSE of 400, we would estimate that the standard deviation is 20 units. However, this approach has a number of limitations, which cause it to underestimate the future variation in demand and hence lead to safety stocks that are too low, resulting in poorer service than we intended. There are three reasons for this:

1. As we saw in Chapter 3, if we use the RMSE from the in-sample periods (i.e., the fitting periods), this will tend to underestimate typical forecast errors because we estimated the parameters of our method already knowing what the actual sales figure are. In the future, the underlying circumstances may change, so our forecasting model will be less accurate than it was in the past. In addition, the past data that we had access to may have caused us to estimate a wrong model.

2. Even if we use the RMSE for the hold-out sample, this will still tend to underestimate the standard deviation. We may have too few forecasts for the hold-out periods to get a reliable estimate of forecast accuracy. The true extent of variation of actual sales around the point forecast – including unusually large errors – is unlikely to be seen in a small sample of forecasts.

3. The RMSE may only be measured for one-period-ahead forecasts, but the lead time might be a multiple or fraction of the typical period. For example, the RMSE may show accuracy of one-month-ahead forecasts, but the lead time might be 2.5 months. Rescaling the RMSE to its equivalent for the lead time period is not easy because sales figures and forecast errors are likely to be autocorrelated.

(In contrast, if the forecasts we have used to measure the RMSE are biased, this will overestimate the standard deviation; but then, of course, our estimate of expected sales will be awry.)

If you suspect your software is basing its forecasts of required safety stocks on the RMSE, then you should be prepared to see stock-outs occurring more often than they should. If you know the number of unfulfilled orders, it is probably worth monitoring how often stock-outs occur and working out what increase in safety stock would have reduced their frequency. If this will take too long before you get results, an alternative would be to look at the indications of required safety stock that the forecasting system made in the past and see how much of an increase would have reduced them to the desired frequency. At any rate, some upward tweaking of the indicated safety stock level will probably be beneficial.

More sophisticated and more up-to-date software products are able to make better estimates of the safety stock you'll need. But, of course, even these are not perfect. Exceptionally high sales that don't fit the historical pattern and changing underlying conditions can impede the accuracy of the computer's indications. Again, the tendency is to underestimate required safety stocks. However, the computer-based indications are likely to be much more reliable than those based purely on management judgment.

7.3.1   Using Prediction Intervals to Determine Safety Stocks

Some software products do not suggest safety stock levels, but they do produce forecasts in the form of prediction intervals. A prediction interval is a range of demand, such as 90 to 110 units, that has a given probability of capturing the actual demand. For example, a 95% prediction interval of 90 to 110 units should have a 95% chance of including the actual demand in its range. The 95% is called the *coverage probability*. Here it implies there is a 1 in 20 chance that the actual demand will fall outside the range. More specifically, if the forecast errors follow a normal distribution, there is a 2.5% chance that actual demand will be *above* the upper limit of the interval. Thus, if we hold stocks of 110 units at the start of the lead time, there will be a 2.5% (i.e., 1 in 40) chance that we will have a stock-out.

While some software products will provide a prediction interval to suit your purposes, others tend only to provide 95% intervals, or intervals with other standard probabilities like 90% or 99%. This means that, if your software only provides you with a 95% interval and you use its upper limit to determine your reorder level, then you are stuck with a 2.5% probability of a stock-out. However, the following procedure uses the information in a prediction interval to determine the stock level needed to achieve any level of customer service. It assumes that the prediction interval is for the lead time and not some other period and that the forecast errors are normally distributed.

1. Calculate the width of the interval, then halve this.

2. Divide the half-width by the appropriate value of the conversion factor, K, from Table 7.2. This will give you an estimate of the standard deviation.

3. Your reorder level $=$ expected sales $+ Z \times$ standard deviation (where the appropriate value of Z can be found in Table 7.1 or published tables of the normal distribution).

For example, suppose your software provides a point forecast of 500 units for the demand in the lead time and a 95% prediction interval of 400 to 600 units. You want to limit the probability of a stock-out during the lead time to 1%. The interval is 200 units wide, so the half-width is 100 units. Because this is a 95% interval, we divide this by 1.96 (from Table 7.2) to obtain an estimate of the standard deviation of $100/1.96 = 51$ units. The appropriate value of Z from Table 7.1 is 2.33, so the reorder level needs to be set to:

$$500 + 2.33 \times 51 = 619 \text{ units}$$

which involves a safety stock of 119 units.

Table 7.2 Conversion Factors for Standard Prediction Intervals

Interval	K
80%	1.28
90%	1.65
95%	1.96
99%	2.58

7.4 WHAT IF THE PROBABILITY DISTRIBUTION OF DEMAND IS NOT NORMAL?

Our analysis so far has assumed that demand during the lead time follows a normal distribution. A normal distribution is an abstract mathematical model. For example, it has no upper or lower bounds, so it assumes that infinite demand, both positive and negative, is possible. It is also known as a continuous distribution because it assumes that products can be sold in infinitely divisible quantities – for example, 8.23412 fan heaters. Demand will never exactly conform to the normal distribution, but it can provide a good approximation in many practical contexts. This is likely to be true when products sell in large numbers and the probabilities of demand exceeding, or falling below, the point forecast are roughly the same. However, in some cases the normal distribution is not appropriate. We next look at some commonly used alternatives.

7.4.1 The Log-Normal Distribution

A typical log-normal distribution of lead time demand is shown in Figure 7.3. Here the distribution is highly skewed and, while relatively low levels of demand are most frequent, there is a possibility of very high levels occurring. Like the normal distribution, the distribution is continuous. When we have intermittent demand, the size of orders in periods *when they do occur* can sometimes be modeled by a log-normal distribution.

If your software provides a standard prediction interval for demand in the lead time, such as a 95% interval, as before this may not be consistent with your desired service level. However, when a log-normal distribution applies, you can use the interval to determine the reorder level needed to meet your service level by applying the following steps:

1. Take the natural logarithm of the upper and lower limits of the interval (the natural logarithm can be found on many calculators using the "ln" button, or you can use the LN() function in Microsoft Excel).

2. Calculate the halfway position between these two logs. Call this M.

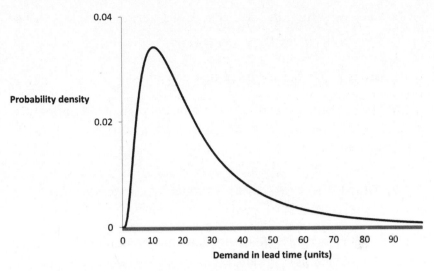

Figure 7.3 A log-normal distribution of demand

3. Find the difference between the two logs and divide it by two.

4. Divide the half-width by the appropriate value of the conversion factor, K, from Table 7.2. Call this value S.

5. Calculate: $X = M + Z \times S$ (where the appropriate value of Z can be found in Table 7.1 or published tables of the normal distribution).

6. Your reorder level $= e^X$ (the e^x button can be found on many calculators or you can use the EXP() function in Microsoft Excel).

For example, suppose your software has used a log-normal distribution and gives you a 95% prediction interval for the demand in the lead time of 3 to 144 units, but you want to allow only a 1% probability of a stock-out.

1. Taking the natural logs of the limits of the interval gives us 1.10 and 4.97.

2. The halfway position between them is 3.04. This is M.

3. The difference between the two logarithms is $4.97 - 1.10 = 3.87$.

4. The half-width is 1.94. Since we have a 95% interval, we divide this by $K = 1.96$ (from Table 7.2). This gives 0.987, which is S.

5. Since we want only a 1% chance of a stock-out, Table 7.1 gives a value of Z of 2.33.

6. Therefore $X = 3.04 + 2.33 \times 0.987 = 5.34$.

7. The reorder level $= e^{5.34} = 209$ units.

This high reorder level reflects the long right tail of log-normal distribution, which implies that we need to allow for the possibility of very high demand.

7.4.2 Using the Poisson and Negative Binomial Distributions

The approximation provided by the normal distribution is likely to be poor when demand for a product is relatively small and it is only sold in whole number quantities. In this case, we need to use a discrete distribution – a distribution that assumes that fractional units cannot be sold. Two such distributions are available in some software products. These are the Poisson and the negative binomial distributions.

The Poisson distribution gives the probabilities that demand in a given period will equal different whole-number quantities. It assumes that the demand occurs randomly over the period in question. To compute the probabilities, we only need to know the mean demand for the period. The standard deviation is equal to the square root of the mean. Figure 7.4 shows a Poisson distribution when the mean demand in the lead time is 3 units. We can obtain the mean using methods such as exponential smoothing when the point forecast will provide the estimate. Notice that, unlike the normal distribution, which is symmetrical, the Poisson distribution is skewed with a long tail to the right. This means that any prediction intervals will not be symmetrical around the point forecast.

For example, the lead time for a product is one month, and demand for the last 10 months is shown in Table 7.3.

The computer made a forecast that the expected (mean) demand in month 11 would be 1 unit (this is the point forecast), and it used the Poisson distribution to produce a 95% prediction interval of 0 to 3 units. Now that we know the forecast of mean demand, the Poisson distribution can also be used to give the probabilities for different

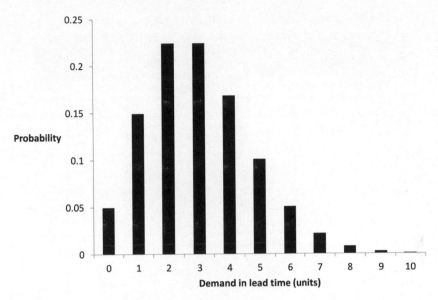

Figure 7.4 Poisson distribution with a mean of 3

Table 7.3 Intermittent Demand with a Poisson Distribution

Month	1	2	3	4	5	6	7	8	9	10
Demand (units)	1	0	1	2	0	1	2	3	0	1

demand levels. From these we can calculate the probability that each demand level will be exceeded. Table 7.4 displays these probabilities.

If we want to achieve a customer service level that allows only a 1% (0.01) probability of a stock-out, we should have a reorder level of 4 units (3 units would give us a 1.9% probability of a stock-out).

Sometimes the variation in demand for low-demand items sold in whole-number quantities is too great for the Poisson distribution to cope with. As we saw, the Poisson distribution assumes that the standard deviation of demand is equal to the square root of the mean demand. When the standard deviation is much greater than this, the negative binomial distribution can be used as an alternative. Figure 7.5 shows a negative binomial distribution with a mean of 3 units and a standard deviation of 3.5 units (note that this is more than double the square root of the mean, which is 1.7 units). It can be seen that the

Table 7.4 Poisson Probabilities for Lead Time Demand

Demand in Lead Time (Units)	Probability	Probability of Exceeding This Demand
0	0.368	0.632
1	0.368	0.264
2	0.184	0.080
3	0.061	0.019
4	0.015	0.004
5	0.003	0.001
6	0.001	0.000

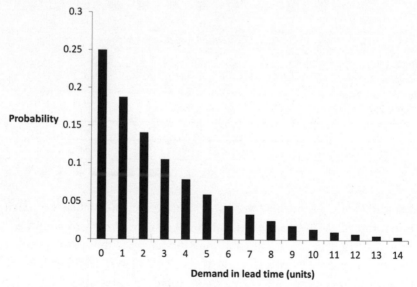

Figure 7.5 Negative binomial distribution with a mean of 3 and standard deviation of 3.5

distribution is highly skewed and any prediction intervals estimated from it are therefore highly asymmetric around the expected sales or point forecast.

For example, the lead time for a product is one week and the sales for the last 10 weeks are shown in Table 7.5.

The computer made a forecast that the expected (mean) demand in week 11 would be 2 units. The negative binomial distribution with

Table 7.5 Intermittent Demand with a Negative Binomial Distribution

Week	1	2	3	4	5	6	7	8	9	10
Sales (units	1	0	6	3	0	4	1	3	0	2

Table 7.6 Negative Binomial Distribution Probabilities for Lead Time Demand

Demand in Lead Time (Units)	Probability	Probability of Exceeding This Demand
0	0.333	0.667
1	0.222	0.444
2	0.148	0.296
3	0.099	0.198
4	0.066	0.132
5	0.044	0.088
6	0.029	0.059
7	0.020	0.039
8	0.013	0.026
9	0.009	0.017
10	0.006	0.012
11	0.004	0.008
12	0.003	0.005

this mean gave a 95% prediction interval of 0 to 7 units. Now that the mean has been forecast we can obtain the probabilities of different demand levels and the chances of these being exceeded (see Table 7.6).

If we want to allow only a 2% (0.02) probability of a stock-out, we should have a reorder level of 9 units (8 units would give a 2.6% probability of a stock-out). Given that the expected demand is only 2 units, this implies 7 units of safety stock, reflecting the fact that demand modeled by the negative binomial distribution is highly variable.

7.5 TEMPORAL AGGREGATION

Sales histories recorded at the daily or weekly level are often highly volatile. They may even show the characteristics of inter-mittent demand with some days or weeks recording zero sales. By aggregating sales from high-frequency time buckets (e.g., days) to lower-frequency buckets (e.g., weeks of months), we can end up with smoother patterns of sales and less uncertainty about future demand, making forecasting easier and more accurate. At least one forecasting product (SAS Forecast Server) will automatically perform temporal aggregation – though in its manual it is referred to as *accumulation*.

Temporal aggregation can be either nonoverlapping or overlapping. To see the difference, look at the sales history in Table 7.7. In nonoverlapping aggregation, we simply sum the sales figures for each week. This leads to a smoother series. However, we now only have 3 observations, rather than 21, so for this method to be useful, we need to have access to long sales histories so that the aggregated series contains enough data to allow appropriate forecasting methods to be applied. The overlapping aggregation in Table 7.7 is a seven-day moving total. On any day, the aggregate figure is the sum of sales in the seven days centered on that day. This gives us more observations, but since most of the daily sales figures are counted more than once in the aggregate series, this may complicate our forecasting process. Note that neither aggregate series contains sales figures of zero.

Once we have our forecast for the aggregate sales, we may need to disaggregate this. For example, for the nonoverlapping series in Table 7.7, suppose we have a forecast for the following week of 8 units, but now need to forecast sales for the individual days in that week. The simplest way to disaggregate the weekly forecasts is to assume that each day will see the same levels of sales. This implies a forecast of $8/7$ units $= 1.14$ units per day. However, if we expect the days to have different levels of sales, we can estimate these by calculating what percentage of the total sales in a week was contributed by each day, and then average the percentages over all the weeks. For example, in week 1, Sunday contributed $4/12 = 33\%$ of the week's sales. In the following weeks it contributed $2/10 = 20\%$ and $0/9 = 0\%$. So, on average, it contributed 17.8% of a week's sales. This gives a forecast for Sunday of 17.8% of $8 = 1.42$ units. Yet another alternative would be to take a weighted average by giving more weight to the more recent percentages, like the 0%, but there is no evidence that this leads to greater accuracy than the simple average.

Table 7.7 Nonoverlapping and Overlapping Temporal Aggregation

Day	Daily Sales	Weekly Sales	
		Nonoverlapping	Overlapping
Sun	4		
Mon	0		
Tue	1		
Wed	5	12	12
Thu	0		10
Fri	2		13
Sat	0		14
Sun	2		9
Mon	3		11
Tue	2		10
Wed	0	10	10
Thu	2		8
Fri	1		7
Sat	0		6
Sun	0		10
Mon	2		8
Tue	1		8
Wed	4	9	9
Thu	0		
Fri	1		
Sat	1		

Research suggests that temporal aggregation can be beneficial in improving forecast accuracy. The reduction in the number of observations available to the forecasting method is outweighed by the reduced volatility and uncertainty associated with the forecasts. For example, suppose that you need a forecast for the period covered by your lead time – say this is three months – but your sales history is recorded for single months. It is usually better to aggregate the sales history first, so it is in three-month buckets, and then forecast. Forecasting the monthly series and then adding three months' worth of forecasts is likely to be less accurate. If you don't have to align the bucket with a particular lead time, research suggests that the higher the level of aggregation, the greater the benefits that will ensue.

7.6 DEALING WITH PRODUCT HIERARCHIES AND RECONCILING FORECASTS

Often we need to forecast sales at different levels of aggregation. For example, a vehicle manufacturer may need to forecast the monetary value of its total sales, the value of sales in each product class (cars, van, and buses), and the value of sales within each class (e.g., by models of car). Alternatively, total sales may be disaggregated by markets (e.g., domestic versus business) or region (e.g., by country and then by regions within a country). Together, the sales at different levels of aggregation form a hierarchy.

The problem is that if we make separate forecasts for each level of the hierarchy, it is unlikely that the forecasts will be consistent. Add up the individual forecasts of sales of cars, vans, and buses, and they will almost certainly be different from a separate forecast of total sales. Reconciliation methods attempt to address this problem. Three methods available in many software products are bottom-up, top-down, and middle-out forecasting.

7.6.1   Bottom-Up Forecasting

In bottom-up forecasting, we simply produce a separate forecast for each item at the lowest level of the hierarchy (e.g., for each car model). These are then summed to give forecasts for the categories at the level above (e.g., total sales of cars). We carry on the process of summing until we obtain a forecast for the item at the top of the hierarchy (e.g., total company sales for all vehicles).

The advantages of bottom-up forecasting are as follows:

1. *Forecasting for the individual items at the lowest level of the hierarchy allows the forecasts to take into account conditions that are specific to each item.* For example, a particular model of sports car may have suddenly become fashionable after its appearance in a block-buster movie, so there is a recent upward trend in its sales. This

may contrast with a general downward trend of vehicle sales. Similarly, we can model the idiosyncratic seasonal patterns of individual products.

2. *We can incorporate local knowledge into a forecast.* For example, the managers of an individual supermarket can build their expertise on their local market into the forecast. Staff at the head office are unlikely to have this knowledge.

However, bottom-up forecasting also has three disadvantages:

1. *Sales for individual products may be volatile or intermittent, or sales histories may be short.* This makes it difficult to obtain reliable estimates of trends or seasonal patterns or to identify the most appropriate forecasting method for each sales time series.

2. *It might be difficult to detect relationships between potential sales drivers and the sales of an individual product.* For example, leading indicators, such as rises in interest rates, may impact on sales, but the relationship between interest rates and the sales might be hard to see, whereas the relationship between the indicator and company-wide sales may be more evident. Thus, forecasts based on methods like regression analysis may not be feasible in bottom-up forecasting.

3. We regularly need to make separate forecasts for each item at the lowest level of the hierarchy. This can be demanding if the number of these items is large.

7.6.2 Top-Down Forecasting

Top-down forecasting dispenses with the need to make lots of individual-item forecasts. Instead, a forecast is made for the category at the top of the hierarchy, and this is then divided up to reflect the relative sales levels of the lower-level items. There are several ways of carrying out the division into separate forecasts.

In the first method, called *average historical proportions*, we calculate for each past period what proportions of total sales were contributed by each individual item. Then we average these proportions. Table 7.8 shows a simple example where we have data for just four past periods

Table 7.8 Average of Historical Proportions

Product	Periods				Average Proportion
	1	2	3	4	
A	0.1	0.2	0.1	0.4	0.200
B	0.4	0.3	0.4	0.3	0.350
C	0.3	0.3	0.4	0.1	0.275
D	0.2	0.2	0.1	0.2	0.175
Total sales $	150,000	222,000	210,000	460,000	

and four products. For example, in period 1, Product A accounted for 0.1 (or 10%) of a company's total sales of $150,000, while Product B accounted for 0.4 of total sales, and so on. The last column is a simple average of these proportions and we can use this to divide up any future forecast of total sales.

The second method simply involves summing the sales of each individual product over all available past periods and dividing this by the total sales over these periods. Table 7.9 shows an example, using the same data as in Table 7.8. For example, Product A had total sales over the four periods of $264,400 while all four products collectively generated sales of $1,042,000 over these periods. So Product A's sales contributed 0.254, or 25.4% of this total. These proportions could be used as an alternative to those in Table 7.8 when splitting a total sales forecast between the products.

Which approach to determining proportions is best? Currently, there is no clear evidence, but the first method has the advantage that we can forecast the proportions themselves. This means that we can,

Table 7.9 Sales of Individual Products and Their Proportions of Total Sales

Product	Periods				Total Sales $	Proportion
	1	2	3	4		
A	15,000	44,400	21,000	184,000	264,400	0.254
B	60,000	66,600	84,000	138,000	348,600	0.335
C	45,000	66,600	84,000	46,000	241,600	0.232
D	30,000	44,400	21,000	92,000	187,400	0.180
					1,042,000	

for example, give more weight to more recent proportions than older ones and hence respond to changes in the relative contributions of different products. However, more research is needed to establish the effectiveness of this approach.

The advantages and disadvantages of top-down forecasting are the opposite of those of bottom-up forecasting. In particular, top-down forecasting has the disadvantage that we don't use knowledge about the sales patterns of individual products. It also has an additional disadvantage. Researchers have shown that, even if the top-level forecasts are unbiased, the forecasts for the lower level items are bound to be biased.

7.6.3 Middle-Out Forecasting

This is a compromise between top-down and bottom-up forecasting. We produce forecasts for each of the categories in the middle level of the hierarchy (or any level other than the top or bottom). We then sum these to get forecasts for the level above (in the same way as for bottom-up forecasting). We also disaggregate each middle level forecast to give forecasts for the items that are below them in the hierarchy (as with top-down forecasting). The advantage is that sales histories at a middle level are likely to be less volatile than those at the lowest level, but they may retain some of the particular characteristics of the lower level series that will be lost at a higher level. However, as with top-down forecasting, when we disaggregate the forecasts from the middle level to lower levels, our forecasts at these levels are bound to be biased.

7.6.4 Hybrid Methods

With some software products it may be possible to use a hybrid method to obtain forecasts for hierarchies. For example, we may have a situation where all of our products have the same seasonal pattern, but the trends of the individual products vary. In this case, it make sense to estimate the seasonal pattern at the top of the hierarchy because the volatility and noise of the sales of the individual products is likely to be "averaged out," so we will get more reliable estimates of the seasonal indices. Estimating the seasonal pattern in this way is also sensible when the sales histories of some of the individual products are short. However, to estimate the levels and trends, we would need to focus on the individual product sales histories. A typical procedure involves the following steps:

Step 1. Aggregate all of the sales to the top level of the hierarchy.

Step 2. Apply a seasonal forecasting method, such as the Holt-Winter's method, to the aggregate sales series. This will produce estimates of the seasonal indices that can be applied to all the products.

Step 3. Deseasonalize the sales histories of the individual products by using the seasonal indices (see Chapter 2).

Step 4. Use nonseasonal forecasting methods on each of these deseasonalized series (e.g., simple exponential smoothing or Holt's method) to obtain estimates of their level and, if appropriate, their trend. Use these to produce forecasts for each product.

Step 5. Reseasonalize the forecasts using the seasonal indices for the aggregate series obtained at Step 2. For additive seasonality, this will involve adding the seasonal index to the deseasonalized sales. For multiplicative seasonality, it will involve multiplying the deseasonalized sales by the seasonal index.

7.6.5   Issues and Future Developments

It can be seen that none of the aforementioned methods of dealing with product hierarchies is perfect. Each has disadvantages, and there is no clear evidence on which method is best. The most accurate approach in any specific situation can only be found by trial and error. In addition, the methods are designed only to produce point forecasts – the issue of how to generate reconciled forecasts in the form of prediction intervals is a topic currently being explored by researchers. Any prediction intervals currently presented by commercial software packages are therefore only approximations.

One development that may soon be implemented in commercial software uses a new approach called *optimal reconciliation*. This revises forecasts at each point in the hierarchy by taking a weighted average of all the other forecasts in the hierarchy. The weights are estimated using linear regression. This method has the advantages that it uses more information than others, ensures that all the forecasts add-up consistently, and guarantees that all the revised forecasts are unbiased, as long as the original forecasts meet this condition. Early tests suggest that the method also produces forecasts that are more accurate.

7.7 WRAP-UP

1. Forecasts can provide guidance on when to order new supplies to replenish stocks of items. However, a point forecast alone cannot provide this guidance. We also need to know the amount of uncertainty associated with the forecast. This is represented by a probability distribution. The normal probability distribution is assumed most often, but other distributions, such as the log-normal, Poisson, and negative binomial distribution are more appropriate in some circumstances.

2. Forecasting packages will generally either use one of these distributions to calculate directly the stock needed to achieve a given customer service level or use the distribution to supply a forecast in the form of a prediction interval. We can use the prediction interval to determine how much safety stock is needed as long as we know the probability distribution that was used to obtain it.

3. Some forecasting packages have a tendency to underestimate the level of uncertainty associated with future demand. Some widening of the prediction intervals provided may be needed, possibly based on their past performance.

4. More accurate forecasts can often be obtained by aggregating sales data into longer periods (e.g., from days into weeks).

5. When products form hierarchies, the forecasts at different levels are rarely consistent. A number of reconciliation processes are available, such as top-down and bottom-up forecasting. However, these methods have their limitations, and improvements to hierarchical forecasting is a topic of ongoing research.

7.8 SUMMARY OF KEY TERMS

Safety (or buffer) stock.	The stock we hold at the start of a period to cater for above-expected demand.
Stock-out.	A situation where demand in a period exceeds the available stocks. It is not necessarily the same as running out of stock. This can happen where demand is exactly equal to the available stock, so no customers are disappointed.
Reorder level or reorder point.	This is used when we continuously monitor our stock levels. It is the level where our stock has depleted to the point where we should place an order for new supplies.
Lead time.	The time between placing an order for new supplies and receiving them.
Periodic review system.	A system where, rather than continuously monitoring our stock levels, we only review them at fixed periods of time, such as once a week or once a quarter.
Customer service level.	This can be defined in many different ways. For our purposes it is the probability of a stock-out that we are prepared to accept.
Standard deviation.	A measure of the spread of a probability distribution.
Prediction interval.	A range of possible future sales levels that has a stated probability of capturing the actual sales between its lower and upper limits. The stated probability is called the coverage probability – values of 95% or 99% are typically produced by forecasting software.
Temporal aggregation.	The accumulation of sales in high-frequency periods (e.g., days) into lower-frequency periods (e.g., weeks). The aim is to get a smoother sales history and to reduce the occurrence of zero sales in the history.

Bottom-up forecasting.	The aggregation of sales forecasts at the lower level of a product hierarchy into categories at higher level. For example, sales forecasts of individual products may be aggregated into sales forecast of types of products and these, in turn, may be aggregated to get a forecast of a company's total sales.
Top-down forecasting.	A process that involves making a sales forecast at the highest level of a product hierarchy (e.g., a forecast of total company sales) and then disaggregating this to obtain forecasts at the lower levels (e.g., forecasts of sales of individual products).
Middle-out forecasting.	A process where sales forecasts are made for categories at a middle level of a product hierarchy. These are then aggregated to get forecasts at higher levels and disaggregated to get forecasts for lower levels of the hierarchy.

7.9 REFERENCES

Boylan J. (2010). Choosing levels of aggregation for supply chain forecasts. *Foresight*, **18**, 9–13.

Hyndman R. J., and Athanasopoulos, G. (2014). Optimally reconciling forecasts in a hierarchy. *Foresight*, **35**, 42–48.

Syntetos, A. (2014). Forecasting by temporal aggregation. *Foresight*, **34**, 6–11.

CHAPTER 8

Automation and Choice

8.1 INTRODUCTION

Even if you are using the most sophisticated forecasting software, you will still have to rely on your judgment to make some decisions. You will need to decide how much sales history to feed into the computer – often, companies retain only short sales histories, which will restrict the range of forecasting methods that can be used. You will also need to decide how sophisticated you want the forecasting method to be. The forecasts of more sophisticated methods may lack credibility amongst managers who do not understand their rationale. Alternatively, their lack of transparency may cause people to have unwarranted faith in their forecasts because they believe that complexity equates to accuracy. Complex methods may also require the collection of costly extra data. If you are using a method like multiple regression, you will also need to decide which predictors might be potentially useful in forecasting sales. For example, you may decide to have a list of candidates that includes advertising expenditure, price, competitors' action, and weather variables, but you will also need to consider whether you can accurately predict these for the period you are forecasting.

This chapter will provide guidance when you face these sorts of choices. For example, we will look at how much past data you need to apply different forecasting methods and ask whether more complex forecasting methods tend to be more accurate.

While there is always a need for judgment, many forecast software products allow you to automate some of the stages of the forecasting process. For example, in some packages you can choose to use their built-in expert systems that will automatically choose a forecasting method for you and give you reasons why they selected that method. If you are using regression analysis, many packages offer an automated way of selecting the best model from the list of potential predictor variables that you have supplied. Some packages will automatically identify outliers and modify these where this is appropriate, or they will automatically detect when older data is no longer useful because there has been a fundamental change in underlying conditions. If you have thousands of forecasts to make on a regular basis, then you will probably have no choice but to automate much of the forecasting task. However, if you do have a choice, we will look at when it is best to rely on automation and when it is best avoided.

8.2 HOW MUCH PAST DATA DO YOU NEED TO APPLY DIFFERENT FORECASTING METHODS?

If you are choosing your own forecasting method, the list of possible options will depend on how much past data you have available. Almost always, more past data is better than less. The only exception is where there has been a fundamental change that renders some past data irrelevant and likely to distort any upcoming forecasts. However, it is important to emphasize that the change has to be *fundamental*. Companies too often ditch past data that could have enhanced their forecasts. I have heard managers say that they only retain three years of data because "if we go back too far, the trends are different." We saw in earlier chapters that methods like exponential smoothing can adapt to changes, and these methods thrive on more data. These days, data storage is cheap, so the advice is to keep hold of your sales history going back as far as you can.

However, what if you only have access to a relatively short sales history – perhaps because a product has not been on the market for long? One option is to use a sales history that is available for an analogous product that has been around for a longer period of time (see Chapter 10). If this isn't available, then the minimum sales history you'll need depends on (1) the complexity of the method you are intending to use; and (2) the amount of randomness in your data.

We can measure the complexity of a method by the number of parameters we need to estimate from the sales history. For example, to apply simple exponential smoothing, we have to estimate not only the value of the smoothing constant but also the starting value for the level (i.e., the initial forecast), so that's two parameters. For Holt's method, we have to estimate its two smoothing constants and the starting values for both the level and trend, so that's four parameters. To fit a straight line, Sales = $a + b$ Time, we need to estimate two parameters, a and b.

It is essential that the number of data points exceeds the number of parameters we need to estimate. If this isn't the case, then any prediction interval would have infinite bounds – suggesting, in theory, that we need to hold infinite safety stocks. The reason for this is that the computer will have no information left to estimate the likely variation of demand around the point forecast.

This suggests that to fit a straight line to a sales history, we need more than two past observations – so three is the absolute minimum. Figure 8.1 shows a straight line fitted to just three sales figures. Suppose that the line is an accurate representation of the trend in sales. It can be seen that the sales exhibit little randomness – the figures hardly deviate from the fitted line. In this case, despite the very short sales history, extrapolating the line will give reliable forecasts for future weeks. Figure 8.1b shows what could happen if the sales

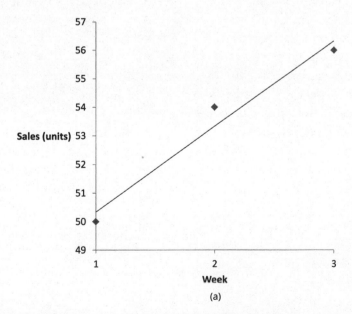

(a)

Figure 8.1a Fitting a line to three observations with little randomness

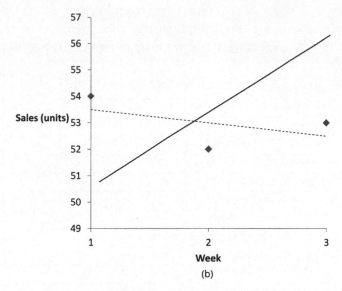

Figure 8.1b Fitting a line to three observations with much randomness

exhibited much greater randomness. The sales have large deviations from the true line (the solid line), and, as a result, the fitted line (the dashed line) grossly misestimates the trend – even estimating it to be negative.

Table 8.1 shows the minimum number of observations needed to apply different forecasting methods, but it is important to stress that these assume that there is virtually no randomness in the data, which is seldom the case. In reality, they are technical minima that are sufficient for the software to work, but they are unlikely to lead to reliable forecasts in most practical situations.

How many more observations do you need to deal with randomness? It is difficult to give a hard-and-fast rule, but one aim will be to have sufficient observations to obtain a prediction interval that is narrow enough to be of practical value. If an interval is excessively wide, it implies that you need to hold very large safety stocks. The width of the interval is proportional to the square root of the number of observations, so if you have four times more observations, you will halve the width of the interval. Double the number of observations, and you will reduce the interval's width by nearly 30%.

Table 8.1 Absolute Minimum Number of Observations to Apply Forecasting Methods

Method	Minimum Number of Data Points
Fitted straight line	3
Quadratic curve	4
Exponential curve	3
Simple exponential smoothing	3
Holt's method	5
Damped Holt's method	6
Holt-Winters method (monthly)	17
Holt-Winters method (quarterly)	9
ARIMA(1,0,0) or ARIMA(0,0,1)	3
ARIMA(1,1,0) or ARIMA(0,1,1)	4
ARIMA(0,1,1)(0,1,1)$_{12}$	16*
ARIMA(0,1,1)(0,1,1)$_{4}$	8*

*Assumes a constant is estimated except where indicated with

8.3 ARE MORE COMPLEX FORECASTING METHODS LIKELY TO BE MORE ACCURATE?

There is no guarantee that choosing a more complex forecasting method will lead to greater accuracy, either in the case of a specific forecast or over a large number of forecasts. Complex methods can handle more elaborate patterns in past data, but they may also have a greater tendency to overfit this data (see Chapter 3). As a result they don't generalize well from the specific pattern observed in the past to patterns that might occur in the future. Even if a more sophisticated method could guarantee increased accuracy, the benefits of this might not outweigh greater data collection and modeling costs and a reduction in transparency.

Often, it turns out that highly sophisticated methods proposed in the research literature have not been adequately tested on out-of-sample data. In some cases, their proponents also neglected to compare their performance with an obvious benchmark – the accuracy of existing simple methods. When two researchers, Scott Armstrong and Kesten Green, reviewed 32 papers that had made this comparison, they found that the accuracy of the more complex methods on hold-out samples was actually worse than those of simpler methods. The famous M-competition, which involved comparing the accuracy of a range of univariate forecasting methods on a 1,001 different time series, reached a similar conclusion.

Armstrong and Green said, "Forecasters should use simple methods – no more complex than is needed for accuracy and usefulness." This advice, of course, does not rule out the use of relatively complex methods when they are appropriate. If you look at hourly electricity demand data, you will find that it has multiple cycles – daily, weekly, and seasonal. It would clearly make no sense to fit a simple straight line through the data to forecast hourly demand for the next month. We need a method that is complex enough to estimate those cycles – but as soon as the complexity of the method has reached a level that is sufficient to achieve accuracy and usefulness, it would be pointless, and possibly damaging, to increase it.

8.4   WHEN IT'S BEST TO AUTOMATE FORECASTS

When software has an automated system that will choose a forecasting method and its parameters, based on the characteristics of a product's sales history, should you use it, or would you do better off choosing the method yourself? There are several advantages to automation.

1. *It saves time when you have large numbers of forecasts to make.* Many organizations regularly have to produce thousands of demand forecasts for items that they sell. Clearly, there is not time for forecasters carefully to review the sales history of each item and fit an appropriate model or method. In this case, the best policy is automation in tandem with management by exception – getting the system to flag products where the forecasts appear not to be performing well. This allows forecasters to focus on investigating the cause of the problem for these special cases.

    To support this, some software products provide a tracking signal. This monitors the forecast errors and cumulates them. If the forecasts are unbiased, the positive errors will tend to cancel out the negative. However, if the forecasts are consistently underestimating or overestimating demand for a product, then the cumulative errors will increase or decrease to a point where they trigger a signal, indicating that there may be a problem with forecasts for that product. This may suggest, for example, that a smoothing constant in exponential smoothing needs to be increased manually because the forecasts are insufficiently responsive to a new situation. Alternatively, it may signal the need to manually switch to a method that can handle upward or downward trends. In some cases, software products will also alert users when an individual forecast error is outside a tolerance threshold.

2. *Good-quality expert systems will tell you why they chose a method.* When the automatic selection is carried out by a good-quality expert system, the choice of method is likely to be based on sound objective principles. Moreover, the system will provide an explanation of why it selected a certain method. For example, it may report that there was too little data available to use method A and that, as no seasonality was evident, it chose method B to produce the forecasts. With judgmental selection, there is a danger that we may see trends or seasonal patterns in data that are not there – or we may miss subtle autocorrelations in sales histories – and, as a result, choose inappropriate methods.

3. *It avoids judgmental forecasting by the back door.* A danger of allowing people to choose the method themselves is that managers may be tempted to manipulate the software until they get the result that they want. This may particularly be the case when the forecaster is subject to political pressures. Even though the forecasts may appear to be generated objectively by the software, in reality they are judgmental forecasts made through the back door. Figure 8.2 shows how this might be done. Figure 8.2a shows the computer's automatically generated forecasts based on simple exponential smoothing. But in the eyes of the sales manager, there's a problem. The forecasted increase in sales for week 37 does not look very impressive, especially since the latest sales were higher than the forecast. So the sales manager ramps up the smoothing constant of the method to make the forecasts more responsive to the latest figures (Figure 8.2b). However, the past forecasts

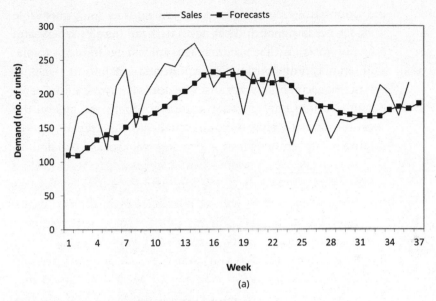

Figure 8.2a The computer's original forecast

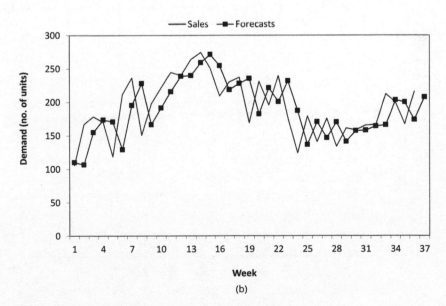

Figure 8.2b Increasing the responsiveness of the forecasts

are now zigzagging all over the place, so they look unreliable and, for the latest week, they forecast a fall in sales when sales actually got a rise. Senior managers won't be impressed. The sales manager then tries fitting a regression line to the time series (Figure 8.2c). That's even worse – it shows a long-term decline in the underlying sales pattern. Finally, he hits on the solution. Just fit a regression line to the last eight weeks' figures (Figure 8.2d). This suggests a pleasing week-on-week climb in the underlying sales pattern. It indicates that 210 units will be sold in week 37, and that's the forecast he chooses to circulate to other managers, who will use it to make plans for next week.

In a pharmaceutical company I visited, managers routinely manipulated computer forecasts in this way. They said they liked the forecasting software that they had bought precisely because it made it easy to play around with the method that generated the forecasts until you got the result you wanted. Conveniently, they still referred to the modified output as the

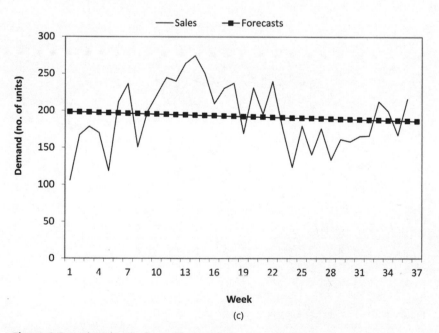

(c)

Figure 8.2c Changing the forecasting method

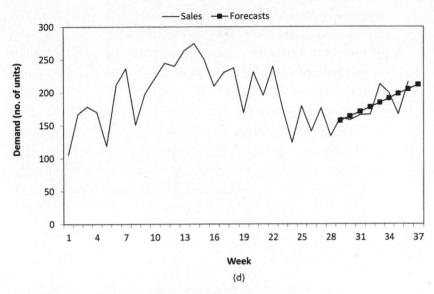

Figure 8.2d   Changing the amount of past data used

"computer-system forecast." This meant that they could blame the software if their forecast had a large error. If you genuinely think that the computer forecast is wrong and have strong evidence to support this, then it is best to be honest and directly replace it with a judgmental forecast, ideally documenting the reasons for your intervention. All of that manipulation can waste a lot of time.

8.5   THE DOWNSIDE OF AUTOMATION

Automation is not without its disadvantages:

1. *The selected forecasting method may lack transparency*. If the automated process chooses a method that no one understands, or if the rationale underlying a forecast is not clear, then the forecast may lack credibility. As a result, there's a danger that it will be replaced by a judgmental forecast when a more understandable statistical forecast would have led to greater accuracy.

2. *Automation should be used with great care when using regression models*. As we saw in Chapter 6, methods such as stepwise

regression are widely available in software products, and they can automatically tell a forecaster which predictor variables to include in their model. However, they suffer from the problems of model selection bias and inconsistency, and many people regard their use as bad practice.

3. *In some circumstances, management judgment may have a useful contribution to make when obtaining forecasts.* We will look at the benefits and dangers of using judgment in forecasting in the next chapter. As we will see, judgment is most likely to be useful when we know that unusual circumstances or special events will be occurring in the future.

8.6 WRAP-UP

1. Forecasting methods usually benefit from having as much past data available as possible. Even if trends in the distant past appear to be different, many methods can adapt to change, and the earlier data could still prove beneficial when forecasting future patterns in demand. When fundamental changes do mean that earlier past data is irrelevant for forecasting, some software products will automatically discount this data, anyway. It is therefore a good idea to retain full sales histories and not to cut these off after a few years.

2. Complex forecasting methods are not necessarily more accurate than simpler methods, and they can be costly to implement. Only use more complex methods when they achieve increased accuracy that justifies any increased costs and when the method is credible and acceptable to forecast users.

3. Automating the forecasting process as far as possible can save time and avoid judgmental biases. It can also prevent judgmental forecasting through the back door. However, the selected methods may lack transparency, and it is not usually advisable to automate the process of choosing a regression model.

8.7 REFERENCES

Armstrong, J. S., and Green, K. C. (2017) Demand forecasting II: evidence -based methods and checklists. https://faculty.wharton.upenn.edu/wp-content/uploads/2017/05/JSA-Demand-Forecasting-89-clean.pdf.

Goodwin, P. (2011). High on complexity, low on evidence: Are advanced forecasting methods always as good as they seem? *Foresight*, **23**, 10–12.

Hyndman, R. J., and Kostenko, A. V. (2007). Minimum sample size requirements for seasonal forecasting models. *Foresight*, **6**, 12–15.

Makridakis, S., and Hibon, M. (2000). The M3-Competition: results, conclusions and implications. *International Journal of Forecasting*, **16**, 451–476.

CHAPTER 9

Judgmental Interventions: When Are They Appropriate?

9.1 INTRODUCTION

Despite what a hardened mathematician might tell you, all forecasts involve judgment to some extent. Even the most sophisticated mathematical models will involve judgment on the choice of forecasting method, how much past data should be used to fit the model, how the accuracy of the model should be measured, and how far ahead it's safe to forecast. However, in this chapter we will focus on another role of judgment – its role in changing or overriding the output of computer-based forecasts.

Researchers have found that such interventions are very common. Managers changed over 90% of their computer-generated demand forecasts in one well-known food company I visited with colleagues. Other companies we visited changed over 60% of their forecasts. Survey after survey has confirmed that managers just cannot keep their hands off the forecasts appearing on their computer screens, despite the time and tedium involved in changing hundreds of forecasts.

So why are people so keen to overrule the indications of their software? There are a number of reasons. Sometimes the computer's forecasts are politically unwelcome. Forecast a downward trend in sales and senior managers might not be too happy, or your department's budget might be cut. Better to adjust the forecasts upwards and hope that your forecasts will be forgotten by the time the actual sales figures arrive.

Alternatively, if forecasting is your job, and every morning you simply print out the computer forecasts and then spend the rest of the day chatting about baseball or reading the newspaper, you might not be in that job for long. Better to make lots of small changes to the forecasts to give the impression that you are adding value to the process. Small changes do not carry much risk, as they cannot do much damage if they take the forecast in the wrong direction. In a study of four companies, we found that the vast majority of changes were very small: 2,456 cartons of butter? No way! I'll make that 2,457.

Another problem is that people sometimes confuse forecasts with decisions or targets, as we saw in Chapter 1. They might add 30% to a reliable forecast of the most likely level of demand, so they have sufficient inventory just in case there's an unexpectedly high demand for a product. There's nothing wrong with that. But it's now a decision on how much to stock. If they still refer to it as a forecast, other managers might think that *it's* the most likely level of demand and make their plans accordingly.

Of course, people often genuinely think they can improve forecast accuracy by overriding the computer. Sometimes they are right and the improvement can be significant. But there's also a danger that they'll be caught up by some well-known psychological biases, so they end up damaging accuracy. In this chapter, we will track down these biases and look at how they can be avoided. We will also identify situations where it is a good idea to intervene and, when this is the case, we will look at ways to make the intervention as successful as possible.

9.2 PSYCHOLOGICAL BIASES THAT MIGHT CATCH YOU OUT

9.2.1 Seeing Patterns in Randomness

We saw in Chapter 2 that data on the demand for a product usually contains random movements that could not have been predicted. Draw a graph of your past sales figures, and these will usually show up as irregular twitches giving the profile of the graph a rough-edged appearance. Because of the impossibility of predicting random events, forecasts should aim only to predict the underlying pattern, or signal, in demand. Forecasting algorithms in most software products are therefore designed to filter out the randomness from past data so that they can detect this underlying pattern. The problem is that, as human beings, we are programmed to search for systematic patterns in anything we come across – including random events.

A year or so ago, I received a tweet containing a graph of prices on the Shanghai Composite stock market index. The tweet showed that, when combined with the lower axis, the graph formed a boundary that was uncannily similar to the border of the US state of Virginia. If you have ever seen faces in clouds or regular sequences in lottery numbers, you are typically human – we are pattern-seeking animals. In forecasting, this means that we often think we have detected patterns that the computer algorithm has missed, and we change its forecast accordingly. When the pattern is illusory, our efforts serve only to reduce accuracy.

We are also story-telling animals. We like to have explanations for the events we witness. So, not only do we often see false patterns in random events, but we are adept at inventing stories to explain these patterns. If there is a random drop in sales from last month, a sales manager won't look too good if he or she can't explain what's happened; so the manager might argue that it must have been caused by a rival company's advertising, or the weather, or the sales staff who have been putting less effort into securing deals with customers.

9.2.2 Recency Bias

Our tendency to be led astray by randomness is related to another bias – recency bias. People tend to focus on the very latest movements in a sales graph. Henry Ford once said, "History is more or less bunk," and forecasters often have the same attitude – discounting the information in their sales history because "back then things were different." "Back then" might refer to periods only a few months back. If a computer-based forecast, which does draw on historic patterns, fails to provide a close fit to recent movements in the graph, it is also discounted and replaced with a forecast that does seem to fit. As a result, people can overreact to a recent freak sales figure, seeing it as a sign of a fundamental change in the pattern of sales. Similarly, low sales last month followed by higher sales this month can be seen as a sign that sales are now on a long-term upward trajectory. But two consecutive numbers don't make a trend; you need a much longer sequence of movements in a given direction to establish that.

Recent patterns in a sales graph are not the only things that can lead to an overreaction. We are also likely to pay undue attention to recent events, particularly those that have high a profile. If a recent sales promotion campaign for a product was a spectacular failure, we may be overly pessimistic when forecasting the sales uplift that another product will achieve when it is promoted, ignoring the fact that most of our promotion campaigns over the years have been successful. Events can attract our attention precisely because they are unusual, but ironically, these events are unlikely occur again. Similarly, events highlighted in the media can also distort our judgments. For example, many people overestimate the risk of being caught in a terrorist attack while they underestimate the risk of less spectacular events that are not usually reported in the media, such as death caused by a fall at home or influenza. Tales in the media of an unlikely product suddenly achieving spectacular sales because of a celebrity-inspired craze might exaggerate the possibility in a manager's minds that their product will be just as successful.

9.2.3   Hindsight Bias

When we look back at past events, they often seem to have been more predictable than they really were. Donald Trump's victory in the 2016 US presidential election, Britain's exit from the European Union – these things don't seem quite so surprising now. They may even seem to have been inevitable. Once an event has occurred, experiments have shown that we can even deceive ourselves into thinking that we correctly predicted that event, when records show that we did no such thing. I have an inkling that I foresaw the international banking crisis of 2008, but nobody I've spoken to can recall me making such a prediction.

This false belief in the accuracy of our past predictions is called hindsight bias, or the "I-knew-it-all-along-effect." It poses a problem for people adjusting computer-based forecasts because it makes them think that they are better forecasters than they really are. As a result, they are likely to be much more willing to overrule the forecasts produced by their software with unjustified confidence that this will improve their accuracy. Our inflated belief in our skills as a forecaster can also make us think that the world is more predictable that it really is, and it can hinder our ability to learn from our past forecast errors.

9.2.4   Optimism Bias

Most people are naturally optimistic. Some people even regard having a sanguine view of the future as a sign of mental health. But, when it comes to adjusting computer-based sales forecasts, optimism can be a problem. People often adjust forecasts in the direction they would like sales to go, usually upwards, even when there's little evidence to support the intervention. In cases where an upward adjustment is justified people can "go over the top" and make a huge adjustment when a more moderate one is appropriate. In a study we conducted of forecasts in three non-retail companies, managers' adjusted forecasts overestimated sales by over 18%, on average. About 30% of the adjustments were in the right direction but were so large that they reduced accuracy. Another 30% of the adjustments were made in the wrong direction – the forecaster increased the computer's forecast when it needed to be reduced, and vice-versa. If you have an incentive in wanting sales to be higher than the computer's forecast, you are likely to pay most attention to any arguments or rumors that are consistent with high sales. Any contrary indicators will probably carry less weight in your judgment.

One of these contrary indicators might be the base rate. The base rate is the proportion of times an event occurs measured over lots of cases. For example, it might tell you that only 30% of new restaurants opened in a city survive for more than a year, or only 40% of advertising campaigns run by a food company have a measurable effect on sales. The problem is that we have a tendency to focus on the specifics of our own situation, causing us to see it as a special case, so we discount the wider perspective provided by the base rate. A new restaurant owner might estimate the probability of his restaurant surviving for more than a year to be 90%. He's hired a good chef, the restaurant is located on a main street, the interior decorations look great, and so on. Of course, these factors may be relevant to how successful the restaurant will be, but the manager should not forget the base rate when estimating the risks of the new business. Similarly, a marketing manager in the food company may focus on the specifics of a forthcoming advertising campaign. Focus groups had a positive reaction to the television commercials, the weather forecast for the campaign period looks encouraging, and a big retailer will be arranging special displays of the product. Again, these factors obscure the depressing base-rate figure, making the manager overoptimistic about the sales uplift the campaign will achieve.

9.3   RESTRICT YOUR INTERVENTIONS

All the evidence from research suggests that people tend to intervene far too often and make too many changes to the demand forecasts produced by their software. These interventions can waste valuable management time – in one company, we estimated that managers spent 80 person-hours each month in meetings devoted to adjusting sales forecasts. Sometimes, the result is only a marginal improvement in accuracy, which may not be justified by the effort and cost involved. In the company in question, half the forecasts were improved at the meetings and half were made less accurate. At worst, these frequent interventions can seriously damage accuracy. This suggests that intervention should be the exception rather than the rule. So how do you know when it is worth intervening?

9.3.1   Large Adjustments Perform Better

An analysis of the adjustments made in the three non-retail companies that we referred to earlier found that only large adjustments tended to improve accuracy. Small adjustments tended to reduce it – though the damage they could cause was, by definition, limited. Changing a forecast from 6,300 to 6,301 units cannot have a big effect on accuracy. The gains achieved through large adjustments are not surprising. Large adjustments can take some nerve. If you increase a computer-based forecast by 80% and this leads to a huge forecasting error, then you could look foolish or incur the wrath of colleagues. This means that they are likely to reflect reliable information that the forecaster has obtained about a forthcoming event that will have a large impact on sales – an event that the software has not taken into account in its forecast. Typical events might be product promotions, price changes, changes in regulations, or the effect of a new government policy or tax rate. However, even with events like these, you need to check that your software does not have a method for incorporating their effects. As we saw in Chapter 2, some software products have built-in facilities for estimating the effect of events like sales promotions.

This raises the question of when an adjustment you are considering is large enough to warrant an intervention. This is likely to depend on the particular forecasting situation – a small adjustment in some contexts may be considered large in others. Nevertheless, it's possible to establish some pointers. First, it's worth doing an analysis of past adjustments to see if they improved accuracy. Is there a cut-off size below which the majority of adjustments worsened accuracy? Second, is the size of your proposed adjustment supported by hard evidence, such as market research? Third, has the forthcoming event that is motivating your proposed adjustment occurred several times in the past – perhaps it's a sales promotion or a price change? If so, did the event tend to have a significant effect on sales? If the effect has been small in the past – say, less than your average forecasting error – it may not be worth making the adjustment, unless you have hard evidence that the effect is likely to be larger this time.

9.3.2 Focus Your Efforts Where They'll Count

I have heard it said that forecasts based on judgment are cheaper to obtain than those generated by computers. In general, this is not the case. Human expertise and time are expensive and scarce commodities. This means that they need to be applied where they will have the greatest benefit. When adjusting computer-based forecasts, this means that people should direct their efforts to the most important products or SKUs.

The ABC method of inventory management involves dividing items into categories A, B, and C, with the A items being the most important and the C items, the least. It reflects the fact that usually a small number of items bring the most value to a company in terms of revenue generation or turnover. For example, just 20% of items may generate 80% of a company's revenue. There are no hard-and-fast rules for the classification but, typically, the A items are the 10% of items that generate 70% of total value; the B items are the 20% of items that generate 20% of total value; and the C items are the remaining items that collectively generate only 10% of total value. In some circumstances, a different measure of importance may be appropriate. For example, in a pharmaceutical company, some drugs may generate relatively little value, but it is crucial that adequate stocks are maintained because they are vital to patients' lives.

It makes sense to concentrate any adjustments on forecasts for the A-category items. But, of course, this should not be a green light for the rampant judgmental adjustment of forecasts for these items. Only items where there are strong indications that adjustment is likely to improve the computer-based forecasts should be considered. Even items where the computer-based forecasts have a history of large errors may not merit intervention. The demand for these items might be inherently unpredictable, and it is likely that any judgmental interference with the computer's forecasts will only make matters worse.

9.4 MAKING EFFECTIVE INTERVENTIONS

As we have seen, adjustments to computer-based forecasts should be made sparingly, but when an adjustment does seem to be justified, what can you do to maximize the chances that the adjustment will be as accurate as possible?

9.4.1 Divide and Conquer

With around 100 billion neurons, each connected to 10,000 other neurons, our brains are the most complex structures in the known universe. We can be brilliant at tasks such as instantly recognizing faces, abstract thinking, speaking and instantly interpreting words, and creative problem solving. But our brains do have their limitations. They have limited computing and processing power – try calculating $(2.3456 \times 8.23412)/45.5643$ in your head – and, according to psychologists, we can only hold a small number of items in our working memory at any one time. This means that if you have lots of information relating to a complex event that is likely to impact on future demand, or if several events may all have an impact at the same time, you might be overwhelmed and struggle to form an accurate estimate of what the effect on demand will be.

In these cases, splitting the problem into smaller manageable parts – bite-size chunks – and focusing on each part separately is likely to improve your judgment. Researchers refer to this as decomposition. For example, suppose that in two months' time you will be running a television advertising campaign to promote one of your products. However, by an unhappy coincidence, the government will be increasing the tax on this product by 5% in the month when your campaign is running. Despite this, a major retailer has agreed to start selling the product for the first time. If you try to estimate in your head the total amount by which the computer-based forecast needs to be changed to reflect all these events, you'll probably have difficulties. It is easier to make a separate estimate of the effect of each event in turn and then sum the results.

Of course, this may not be perfect – one of the events might impact on another so there is an interaction effect and the whole may be greater or less than the sum of the parts. Even so, it is likely to be more accurate than a raw *holistic* judgment. And it comes with other advantages. You now have a documented rationale for your adjustment, which might be useful if you need to defend it at some future date. Other people can see your rationale, potentially allowing them to challenge it and help you to improve the estimate. For some of the separate estimates, you might even have access to hard data, so you will not need to use judgment. Alternatively, you may be able to elicit the input of a specialist. For example, the marketing manager might know that television advertising campaigns for products like this typically generate sales uplifts of 60%.

9.4.2   Using Analogies

When faced with a forthcoming special event, like a product promotion campaign, we might be tempted to try to recall what happened last time we had a promotion. But our memories are fallible, so any adjustment to the computer-based forecast is likely to be unreliable. Worse still, basing the estimate on just one instant of an event is risky – unknown to you, that event may have been subject to unusual circumstances and so is untypical.

Of course, if the forthcoming event is unique – you have never ever run a promotion campaign before – you will not even have one past example to guide you in your judgment. But uniqueness is often in the eye of the beholder. Other companies in your industry – or similar industries – may have experience of promotions and information may be available on their effects. Cast your nets wide enough and you are almost certain to come across many examples of promotions. Your promoted product might be a chocolate bar, but data on the typical promotion effects of all fast-moving consumer goods might still have some value.

In this case, you are making use of multiple analogous events. There is a balance to be struck when choosing analogies, and this choice is usually a judgment call itself. The broader your search for analogies, the more you will capture and the less chance you will have of being misled by a few atypical cases that were affected by freak events. But, as you broaden your search, you will include events that are less similar to your target event – the one for which you have to make a forecast. Sales promotions for breakfast cereals may have different effects than those for chocolate bars. Promotions for household cleaning products may differ even more. Nevertheless, using data obtained from several analogies to guide your judgment is likely to be better than relying on an unsupported wild guess or a single past case that is inaccurately recalled.

9.4.3 Counteracting Optimism Bias

As we saw earlier, people have a predisposition to be overly optimistic. They tend to adjust computer-based forecasts towards sales that are unrealistically high, downplaying any indicators that might disconfirm their beliefs. Optimism bias is so ingrained in our psyche that it is a difficult one to crack, but there are a number of methods that might help to reduce it.

If you make a large number of interventions, monitoring the adjusted forecasts for bias might reveal a consistent tendency to adjust sales forecasts so they are too high. For this, you can use one of the bias measures that we met in Chapter 3, such as the mean percentage error (MPE). Getting feedback on bias is likely to be much more useful than feedback on accuracy because a bias measure tells you what you need to do to if you want to make more effective adjustments in the future. For example, if your adjusted forecasts are, on average, 40% too high, it's clearly worth considering making more moderate upward adjustments. It is important to note that the bias needs to be averaged over several adjustments (as a rough rule, at least the last four adjustments), otherwise you might be overreacting to each random twist and turn in your sales graph. In a survey of forecasting in organizations, we were surprised to find that many companies do not bother to measure the quality of their past forecasts. Yet research suggests that feeding back how well past forecasts performed leads to improvements in the quality of judgmental interventions.

If you do have data on past performance, you can also use the data to mechanically correct any future forecasts. For example if, on average, a forecaster made adjustments in the past that overestimated sales by 45 units, then it's a simple matter to subtract 45 units from all future forecasts. Of course, you need to make sure that this does not lead to forecasts of negative sales in some cases. A more sophisticated method involves using simple regression (see Chapter 6) to estimate the relationship between the actual sales and the forecasts. For example, suppose that fitting a regression line to your last 30 forecasts and actual sales leads to the following equation:

$$\text{Sales} = 25 + 0.6 \times \text{Forecast}$$

This implies that, when you make a forecast of (say) 100 units, you tend to forecast too high because, on average, the actual sales turn out to be only: $25 + 0.6 \times 100 = 85$ units. The original forecast can now be corrected to the new value of 85 units, thereby removing the bias.

The advantage of this method is that it can adapt, depending on the size of the forecast that is made. For example, a manager's high forecasts might have a tendency be too optimistic, but low forecasts might be too pessimistic. In this example, when a manager estimates that next month's sales will only be 10 units, the equation shows that typically sales turn out to be: $25 + 0.6 \times 10 = 31$ units. In this case, the corrected forecast will be higher than the original.

Correcting forecasts may not be appropriate for all circumstances and must be carried out with care. The bias in people's forecasts might improve, or even worsen, over time so you could find that you are correcting for biases that no longer exist or are smaller than they were in the past. Also, if managers find out that their adjusted forecasts are subsequently being corrected, they might react negatively. They could decide to put less effort into the task, reasoning that their forecasts will be changed anyway. Alternatively, they might try to counteract the correction by making their forecasts even more biased. Nevertheless, if we can overcome these difficulties, research suggests that corrections can improve accuracy. Indeed, if a forecaster is open to the corrections, they can be used as a type of feedback on bias, indicating that it might be beneficial to make a change to the forecast they are currently proposing.

In some cases, merely informing people that they tend to forecast too high might not carry much weight. However, reasoned arguments might persuade them that their current forecast needs lowering. In companies, managers often make adjustments to demand forecasts in forecast review meetings. Here a devil's advocate can have a useful role. This is someone who deliberately argues the case that sales will be lower than the level that is currently proposed. If the rationale for the proposed forecast can survive everything the devil's advocate throws at it, then it is probably safe to stay with that forecast. Otherwise, the debate might reveal that the case for a high forecast is weak and unsubstantiated. Of course, debates take time and it's not worth having a devil's advocate challenging hundreds of forecasts. Such challenges will only be worthwhile where the cost of a large forecast error is likely to be significant.

Finally, we saw earlier that optimism bias is often a result of people focusing on a specific case (the inside view) and paying insufficient attention to the underlying base rate derived from lots of similar cases (the outside view). This is another good reason for seeking out analogous cases before making an adjustment. If a sales promotion is forthcoming and similar promotions have on average led to a 30% uplift in sales, then this might moderate a manager's urge to adjust the computer-based forecast upward by 70%, however much he or she thinks the coming campaign is going to be a great one.

9.4.4 Harnessing the Power of Groups of Managers

I have sat in many forecast review meetings involving managers where the current computer-based demand forecast for a given product is projected onto a large screen. The participants discuss, often at length, whether the forecast needs adjusting before moving on to the next product. Assuming that the importance of the forecast justifies it, debate and discussion, involving inputs from managers with different specialities, responsibilities, and knowledge is obviously a good idea. The resulting forecasts are likely to draw on a broader range of information. In addition, debate should ensure that specious arguments for particular forecasts are exposed.

However, reality does not always match this ideal. Research into the way groups actually behave suggests they are often dominated by particular loquacious individuals or members with high status. That serves to limit debate and may deter quieter individuals from making potentially valuable contributions to the discussion.

There are a number of methods designed to harness the power of groups, while avoiding these problems. The most well-known of these is the Delphi method, which was developed at the Rand Corporation in the 1950s. Participants in a Delphi forecasting exercise, or panelists, do not meet face-to-face. Instead, they remain anonymous throughout the whole process. They submit their forecasts (or the adjustments to computer-based forecasts that they think are necessary) to a convenor, ideally together with written reasons to support their estimates. The convenor then calculates statistics to summarize the forecasts. For example, they may state that the median of the adjustments suggested by members of the panel was 2,532 units. These are then sent back to the panel, together with the anonymized written arguments that were received. The members of the panel are then asked to reconsider their original forecast in the light of this information, and the process of collection and summary is then repeated. Usually, the process goes on for two or three rounds of estimation and feedback. The median of the last set of forecasts submitted is then adopted as the group's point forecast. Ideally, members of the panel should be chosen to represent different points of view so that the group starts with a diverse set of opinions.

It can be seen that the Delphi method tries to preserve the sharing of information and exchange of views that goes on in groups, while removing the dangers of face-to-face meetings. Every member's forecast has equal status, regardless of their standing or personality, and in the second, and subsequent, rounds people can change their mind about their forecasts without fear of losing face. However, there is a price to pay. In a well-run face-to-face meeting, there is much more opportunity for the dynamic interchange of information and arguments. Compared to this, the exchanges in a Delphi process are rather pedestrian. In addition, the anonymity of the panelists may encourage them to put less effort into their forecasts. After all, they will get no credit if these forecasts are highly accurate; and, if their forecasts are awry, no one will know who put them forward. Nevertheless, research suggests that, when conducted with care, the Delphi process generally improves the accuracy of forecasts when compared to routine face-to-face meetings.

Prediction markets are a much more recent method for eliciting forecasts from groups of people without the need for them to meet. HP has been prominent in using this method in sales forecasting, and it has launched a commercial product, called BRAIN (Behaviorally Robust Aggregation of Information Networks), to support the wider application of prediction markets. There are several reports that prediction markets have led to more accurate forecasts than the judgmental forecasts of individual experts.

Participants in a prediction market buy and sell assets in the same way that people trade shares on a stock market. For example, an asset may pay out one cent for every unit of a product that is sold this year. If the current market price of the asset is $20 and you believe that sales will reach 4,000 units, then you can buy assets for $20 that you think will be worth $40 by the end of the year. If many other players in the market also decide to buy, then the price will increase. The new price is interpreted as the market's current forecast of the annual sales. For example, if the price rises to $35, this implies a market forecast of 3,500 units.

Unlike Delphi panelists, participants in prediction markets have a financial incentive to think hard about the forecasts. They can also react to new information as it occurs in real time, whereas Delphi panelists can only change their forecasts at the times when they receive a request to reconsider their predictions. However, there is no exchange of reasons and arguments in a prediction market – people simply react to the latest market price. Moreover, falls in this price can lead to cascades when people think the change has occurred because of new adverse information that they are unaware of. Therefore, they decide to sell, which causes further falls in the price. A downward spiral ensues that is unrelated to any real change in the conditions that will affect future sales. Prediction markets also require an investment in additional software to operate the market and update the current asset prices.

9.4.5 Record Your Rationale

Whichever method you use to adjust a computer-based forecast, it is a good idea to record your reasons for making the change. Research shows that this discourages gratuitous adjustments when it is made a mandatory part of the adjustment process. It also has the advantage that you can look back and see which reasons were associated with adjustments that led to improved accuracy and identify those where the adjustment was less successful. Most forecasting software products have a free-form note box for this purpose, but of course, it is important to make the records understandable and clear. In one company I visited, no one could explain the oddly worded and opaque entries in the coded boxes, so the exercise was almost certainly a waste of time.

An alternative to the freeform box is a list of possible reasons for an adjustment, alongside checkboxes that allow the user simply to tick the reasons that are relevant in that case. The lists may contain reasons such as "adjustment for forthcoming sales promotion," "adjustment for change in regulations," 'adjustment for sporting event," "adjustment for price change," and so on. This facility is not available in most commercial software products and so would need to be implemented "offline." The advantage is that the reasons are unambiguous and so can be more easily linked to the subsequent success, or otherwise, of the adjustment. They also make the record keeping less time-consuming. The disadvantage is that they provide a "less rich" account of the rationale for past adjustments.

9.5 COMBINING JUDGMENT AND STATISTICAL FORECASTS

In forecasting, human judgment and statistical algorithms have complementary strengths and weaknesses. As we have seen, humans are subject to psychological biases. They can also be inconsistent, and moods and fatigue can affect the quality of their judgments.

But humans are also adaptable, and they can react quickly to new circumstances or special events. Computer-based algorithms, on the other hand, are consistent and can optimally process large sets of data, but they are less flexible than humans and are less able to handle market intelligence that comes in a qualitative form.

One way of drawing on these complementary strengths is to obtain an independent forecast based on management judgment and an independent computer-based forecast and then simply average the two. For example, if a manager's judgment is that sales will be 50 units next month and the computer algorithm forecasts sales of 70 units, then the average forecast will be 60 units. This is known as combining, and it is an alternative to judgmental adjustment.

A key finding of forecasting research over the last 40 years or so is that combined forecasts are often more accurate than the individual forecasts they are based on. This is because they are able to draw on a wider range of information than the individual forecasts. Also, if one of the forecasts tends to be too high and the other too low, then the average will help to cancel out these biases. To achieve these advantages it is important that the forecasts are made independently. For example, if a manager sees the statistical forecast before producing their judgmental forecast, they may be overinfluenced by it. Usually, a simple average of the two forecasts is sufficient. It might be tempting to consider giving more weight to one of the forecasts, based for example on past accuracy, but it is probably not worth the effort of doing this in most practical circumstances.

While judgmental adjustment is much more common in sales forecasting than combining, some companies have successfully implemented combination as part of their forecasting process. For example, when Brooks Sports, a company that produces high-performance sportswear and accessories, used combining, average sales forecast accuracy improved by 40 percent.

So which process should you use – judgmental adjustment or a combination? We argued earlier that judgmental interventions should usually be the exception rather than the rule. In combining, management judgment will have an effect on every forecast. This means it is likely to be most effective where sales are continuously affected by different special events or where past data on sales is sparse (as with newish products), so the statistical forecast is still relatively unreliable. In some organizations, implementing combining is also likely to be more challenging. As with the mechanical correction of forecasts that we met earlier, it means that people lose control of the final forecast – their judgmental forecasts are now simply an input into a calculation. This may cause resentment and so adversely affect the quality of the judgmental forecasts put forward by managers.

9.6 WRAP-UP

1. Be sparing in your interventions. It's unlikely that you'll have spotted a pattern in past data that the computer has missed.

2. Adjust when you have important and reliable information about a forthcoming special event that the computer-based forecast has not taken into account.

3. Focus on A-category items when considering interventions.

4. Records relating to analogous events can be helpful in providing guidance on what the size of a judgmental adjustment should be. They will obviate the need to rely on memory and may temper any tendency for adjustments to be overly optimistic. Use several analogies where possible.

5. Calculate and monitor the average bias in adjusted forecasts. Use this to assess whether the judgmental adjustments are typically too large or too small, but do not overreact to an isolated biased forecast.

6. If groups of people have to agree on judgmental adjustments, consider using an approach like the Delphi method as an alternative to face-to-face meetings. In some circumstances, prediction markets may also be a feasible alternative.

7. Keep a record of reasons for any interventions.

9.7 REFERENCE

Fildes, R., and Goodwin, P. (2007). Good and bad judgment in forecasting: lessons from four companies. *Foresight: The International Journal of Applied Forecasting*, **8**, 5–10.

CHAPTER **10**

New Product Forecasting

10.1 INTRODUCTION

Making accurate forecasts of the demand for new, or nearly new, products can be challenging. There will be little or no sales history data that we can use for extrapolation or to estimate relationships between sales and predictor variables. In addition, management teams who have invested time and resources in the development of the product may be tempted to make overly optimistic estimates of its chances of success.

Problems like these have led to the development of a range of methods that are intended to improve the accuracy of new product forecasts. For example, intentions surveys involve asking potential customers to indicate the probability that they would buy the new product. Similarly, in choice modeling, potential customers are asked to indicate their preferences between products with different combinations of attributes (e.g., smart phones with different screen sizes, battery discharge times, and prices). The analyst then models customer preferences to estimate the probability that they will choose a particular product in preference to others and, from this, a forecast of the product's market share can be made.

In this chapter, we will focus on the use of statistical time series methods in new product forecasting. When a product has yet to be launched there will, of course, be no demand history to allow the model to be estimated. However, if similar products have been launched in the past, we can fit models to their sales histories and use the forecasts from these as a basis for forecasting the sales of the new product. This is known as forecasting by analogy, or FBA.

Finally, we will look at an alternative approach, diffusion modeling, which can often be applied in sales forecasting software. A diffusion model is intended to reflect the way that the ownership of new products spreads through populations of customers over time, starting with customers who are willing to risk purchasing the new product soon after its launch.

Despite the availability of these methods, surveys suggest that most new product forecasts are based on management judgment. In the next section, we will look at the dangers of relying solely on management judgment to make sales forecasts for new products. However, later on we will show that the appropriate use of judgment in combination with forecasting by analogy can potentially lead to more accurate forecasts.

10.2 DANGERS OF USING UNSTRUCTURED JUDGMENT IN NEW PRODUCT FORECASTING

Many of the cognitive biases we met in Chapter 9 are likely to lead to inaccuracies if we use management judgment to forecast the sales of new products. We saw that we tend to be overinfluenced by recent events, or events that are easily recalled. This means that a recent product flop, or a spectacularly successful launch that is still fresh in our minds, is likely to distort our estimates of how well a new product will perform.

Similarly, optimism bias may prevail if managers tend to focus on the specifics characteristics of a new product: It's been designed by an enthusiastic team; it's the biggest investment we've made in R & D; competing products are nowhere near to being launched; it'll be backed by a huge advertising campaign. As a result, they forget about the base rate, which may show that only 35% of previous launches have led to products with significant sales.

Then there is the problem of advocacy bias. If the forecasts of a proposed new product's sales are prepared by one person or department, but evaluated by others before a decision to launch or continue development is made, there may be a tendency to deliberately overforecast sales. The people preparing the forecasts may anticipate that the evaluators will view their predictions with skepticism and mark down their figures. To preempt this, they might submit a set of inflated forecasts in the hope that the marketing or development of the product will not be canceled.

In Chapter 9, we also saw that biases can emerge when managers meet in groups to make forecasts of sales. People may be reluctant to express their genuine concerns about the new product's prospects, particularly if the group is highly cohesive (so no one wants to rock the boat) and when it has a dominating leader who is a strong supporter of the product. As a result, a phenomenon called *groupthink* can emerge and the resulting forecasts can be unrealistically optimistic.

Finally, people often learn to improve their judgmental forecasts through feedback. But in new product forecasting, the feedback people receive is itself biased. They only get to see the sales of products that make it to market. Obviously, we cannot get feedback on the performance of forecasts for products that never made it.

10.3 FORECASTING BY ANALOGY

10.3.1 Structured Analogies

The process of *structured analogies* can be used to identify appropriate analogous products that already have a sales history and might provide guidance on the sales prospects for the new product. At least one software product has a facility for carrying this out as a seamless part of the forecasting process. If this is not available, the process can be carried out "off line." The process involves the following six steps that use both computer analysis and management judgment:

Step 1. Make a list of candidate products that have characteristics that are similar to the new product. These characteristics might relate to the type of product (e.g., is it an electronic product?), its price range, the time of year it will be launched, the market it is aimed at, its likely lifespan, and its physical appearance (e.g., its color or style).

Step 2. Compare graphs of the sales histories of these products – either as a gallery or by superimposing the histories onto each other. Consider removing any products that have untypical histories.

Step 3. Cluster similar sales histories into groups. Then use judgment to choose the cluster that has a typical pattern that is expected to be closest to that of the forthcoming product.

Step 4. Fit a statistical model to the sales of the products in the chosen cluster. This may involve fitting a separate model for each product and averaging the models' parameter values to get an "average" model. Alternatively, you may be able to find directly a single model that best fits the average sales in each period of the products in the cluster.

Step 5. Use the model to produce forecasts.

Step 6. Judgmentally adjust the model's forecasts if necessary, but bear in mind the caveats referred to in Chapter 9.

10.3.2 Applying Structured Analogies

To demonstrate the process, we will apply it to forecast the sales of an as-yet-to-be launched pharmaceutical product intended to treat a specific allergy.

Step 1. We first select all of the company's products that are intended to treat allergies. Then we restrict our set to those medications that are taken orally (as is the case with the new product) and those that have the same pack size. This leaves seven previously launched products for which we have sales histories for 48 months following launch.

Step 2. The sales of the products are on different scales, with some products selling in hundreds and others in thousands of units. To make their patterns comparable, we will express each month's sales as a percentage of the product's total sales achieved over the 48 months. As can be seen in Figure 10.1, these plots of the percentages look quite chaotic when they are superimposed. Nevertheless, we can see that products A and B instantly achieved high sales in their first couple of months, while the remaining products took a while for their sales to build up. We think that the new product will be more similar to these other products, so we eliminate products A and B. Product G is clearly an outlier, so we also remove it. The graphs hint that the sales of some of the products might have seasonal patterns. We might expect this, for example, where drugs are designed to protect people from allergies to pollen. To keep our illustration simple, this will not be considered here, but software such as SAS® New Product Forecasting can take seasonality into account.

Plotting the cumulative percentage sales for the remaining products gives smoother profiles that are easier to compare. Figure 10.2 shows the resulting plots.

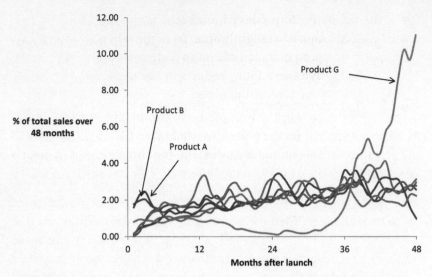

Figure 10.1 Monthly sales of analogous products as percentages of their total sales over 48 months

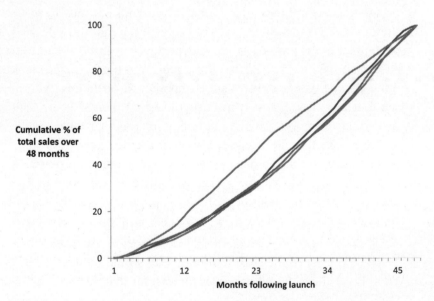

Figure 10.2 Plot of cumulative sales of candidate analogies

Step 3. The remaining four sales patterns look fairly consistent. Though the highest graph is set slightly apart from the others, we think that it also may represent a plausible sales pattern for our new product. So we will leave these four products in the same cluster and use this to obtain our forecasting model.

Step 4. When we average the four products' cumulative percentages for each month, we get the plot shown in Figure 10.3. There is a slight curvature to the cumulative sales, and the computer indicates that a quadratic curve fits the data quite well. This has the formula:

$$\text{Cumulative percentage sales} = 0.93 \,(\text{Month number})$$
$$+ 0.03(\text{Month number})^2$$

where month number is the number of months that have elapsed following the product's launch.

Step 5. We can now use our formula to forecast cumulative percentage sales for the new product for any given number of months following the launch. For example, by the end of month 11 we would expect that the cumulative sales will be: $0.93(11) + 0.03(11)^2 = 13.9\%$ of the total sales we will achieve over the 48 months. Similarly, the formula indicates that by the end of month 12 our sales will have risen to 15.5% of the total. So month 12 will account for 1.6% of the 48 months of sales.

To obtain a forecast of actual monthly sales for each of the 48 months, we need to convert the percentages into sales figures. One way is to obtain an estimate of the first month's sales using judgment or market research data. Assume that this figure is 350 units. Our model tell us that the first month's sales will be $0.93(1) + 0.03(1)^2 = 0.96\%$ of the total sales over the 48 months. So the total sales over these months is $350 \times 100/0.96 = 36{,}458$ units. From this we can now make a sales forecast for any month. For example, earlier we forecast that month 12 would see 1.6% of the 48 months sales. This gives a sales forecast for that month of 1.6% of $36{,}458 = 583$ units.

Step 6. If we had good reason to think that this forecast was too high or low, we could now make a judgmental adjustment to it. For example, our fitted curve in Figure 10.3 looks a little high for the first 12 months so we may wish to lower the forecasts slightly.

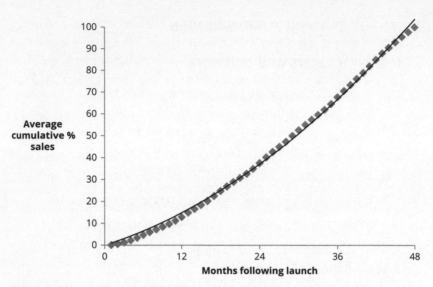

Figure 10.3 Average cumulative percentage sales of four analogous products and fitted curve

The previous procedure can be varied in several ways. At Step 2, if the analogous products have similar levels of sales – rather than, for example, being measured in thousands in some case and hundreds in others – then you can work with the raw sales figures, rather than percentages of the total sales over the periods being forecast. Also, if the graphs of actual monthly sales of the analogous products do not look too chaotic and appear to follow consistent patterns, then there would be no need to work with cumulative sales. Other forecasting methods that appear to be appropriate to the data can also be applied to the analogous time series instead of curve fitting.

The process involves a mixture of judgment and formal analysis and may seem to be relatively crude, but the judgmental inputs are structured, confined to roles where they work best, and informed by the computer analysis. Given the challenges of new product fore-casting, the combination of different methods – in this case, market research, judgment, and statistical analysis – is likely to improve accuracy. In addition, the variation between the curves in Figure 10.2 gives us some idea of the level of uncertainty that is associated with our forecasts.

10.4   THE BASS DIFFUSION MODEL

10.4.1   Innovators and Imitators

The forecasting by analogy we just carried out provides no explanation for the likely future pattern of a new product's sales. We are simply assuming that its sales will imitate patterns we have previously seen. In contrast, the Bass diffusion model, which is available in many forecasting software products, does provide an explanation based on the behavior of different types of potential customers.

When a new product is first marketed, potential customers can be divided into two broad categories. *Imitators* buy the product only after having heard about other people's experience of owning it. In their eyes, this reduces the risk that the product will disappoint them. Alternatively, they may be unaware of the benefits of owning the product until others have told them about it. In contrast, *innovators* are keen to buy the product as soon as they hear about it through advertising or media exposure. They do not wait for reports from other purchasers on how the product has fared.

A Bass model takes into account these different behaviors, and a typical model is shown in Figure 10.4. The left-hand graph shows the number of new people adopting the product in each period after launch, while the right-hand graph shows the cumulative number of adopters over time. This has a typical S-shaped profile. Note that

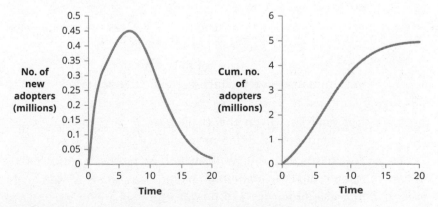

Figure 10.4   A typical Bass model of numbers of adopters over time

individuals become adopters as soon as they make their first purchase of the product. Therefore, the number of units sold may differ from the number of adopters if people make multiple purchases of the product.

The tendency of people to buy the product because of media exposure or advertising is reflected by the coefficient of innovation or p. For example, if $p = 0.1$, it implies that 10% of potential adopters who have yet to buy the product will do so in the forthcoming month or year as a result of media influence. The value of p is always between 0 and 1.

The tendency of people to adopt the product as a result of hearing about other people's purchases, so-called word-of-mouth, is reflected in the coefficient of imitation, q, which also has a value between 0 and 1. As more and more people adopt the product, the power of word of mouth becomes stronger. More people are likely to be recommending it to others, so the rate of adoption of the product begins to accelerate. However, eventually, the total number of adopters will approach the market's saturation point, and it will be more and more difficult to persuade the remaining nonpurchasers, so-called laggards, to buy. This causes growth in the number of adopters to slow until very few new people are taking up the product.

10.4.2 Estimating a Bass Model

The formula for the Bass model is:

   No. of adopters in a period

$= p \times$ No. of potential customers who have yet to adopt at start
   of period

$+ q \times$ Proportion of market who have already adopted at start
   of period

$\times$ No. of potential customers who have yet to adopt at start of period

For example, suppose that we want to forecast the monthly sales of a product for which the market of potential customers is estimated to be 20,000, p is estimated to be 0.1, while the estimate for q is 0.2. At the start of July, 12,000 people have already adopted the product.

This means that 12,000/20,000, that is 0.6 (or 60%) of the market, are already adopters, but we still have 8,000 potential customers who have yet to adopt. The Bass model will therefore forecast that the number of new adopters in July will be:

$$[0.1 \times 8,000] + [0.2 \times 0.6 \times 8,000] = 1,760.$$

To apply a Bass model, you need three estimates – the values of p and q and the total number of potential adopters (i.e., the size of the market). If you already have early sales figures for a new product (e.g., sales for the first few months), then a Bass curve can be fitted to this data to estimate the values of the three parameters. For example, the first 10 months' sales of a new product are shown in Table 10.1 and displayed in Figure 10.5. We will assume that all purchases are made by new adopters and that no one is making multiple purchases.

When software was used to fit a Bass model to the data, it estimated that $p = 0.006$ and $q = 0.679$ and the total market size = 9,574 units (note that estimates can vary, depending on the algorithm used). Figure 10.5 shows the fitted model and its forecasts up to month 16.

Table 10.1   First 10 Months' Sales of a New Product

Month	1	2	3	4	5	6	7	8	9	10
Sales (units)	14	35	91	140	257	410	752	914	1303	1623

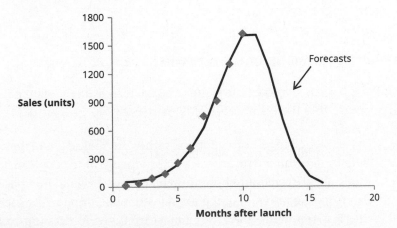

Figure 10.5   Bass model fitted to data

The model suggests that the product will have a short life cycle and that the number of new adopters will be virtually zero after month 16. Note that fitting a model to this small number of data points and then extrapolating it is risky and the forecasts should be treated with great caution. This is especially the case here as the extrapolation is predicting a reversal in the previously observed trend.

If a product has not yet been launched, the values of p and q can be estimated by fitting Bass models to one or more previously launched analogous products. Where several analogies are available, their average p and q values can be used. Alternatively, typical p and q value for particular industries are also available in some publications. However, analogies are likely to have limited use in estimating market size where the scales of their sales vary from that expected for the new product, despite their sales patterns being similar. In this case, estimating the size of the potential market is probably best achieved through consumer intentions surveys, demographic data, or management judgment. However, estimates based on management judgment are likely to benefit from structured decomposition. For example, separate estimates could be made of the percentage of people in different socio-demographic groups who are likely to be potential customers. Where a group of managers has to agree on the estimate, then approaches such as the Delphi method (see Chapter 9) are likely to be effective in eliciting honest opinions and avoiding group pressures.

10.4.3   Limitations of the Basic Bass Model

While the basic Bass model can be an effective forecasting tool in many situations, it does have a number of limitations:

1. It is designed to forecast adoption rather than sales. It will there-fore underestimate future sales for products where people make multiple or repeat purchases or replace their original purchases later on (e.g., they may replace a lost mobile phone). As such, the Bass model is likely to be most useful in forecasting con-sumer durable products, which people tend to buy in single

quantities. When they eventually replace them after long periods of use, they may do so with a different, or more up-to-date, product anyway.

2. In industries where the coefficient of imitation may be increasing (e.g., because the Internet is making word-of-mouth more powerful), it is important to choose recent analogies. Otherwise, q will be underestimated. However, recent analogies may not yet have completed their life cycle, so Bass models fitted to them will be based on incomplete data.

3. The model assumes that the size of the market and p and q will remain unchanged in the future, and it does not take into account variables such as advertising expenditure, price, the actions of competitors, and the probability that the product will become obsolete prematurely. Extensions to the basic model have been developed take into account these factors, but these are not usually available in standard forecasting software products.

4. In some cases, other types of S-shaped curves may provide a closer fit to the cumulative numbers of adopters over time. These include the logistic and Gompertz curves.

5. Not all new products have demand patterns with a single peak like that in Figure 10.4. For example, some products have an early rapid growth in demand, followed by a drop in demand, and then a subsequent recovery to the former peak. None of these S-shaped curves is suitable for modeling patterns like this.

10.5 WRAP-UP

1. New products pose particular challenges to sales forecasters because their sales histories will be short or nonexistent. However, it may be possible to estimate a new product's future sales pattern by analyzing the sales histories of analogous products that have been on the market for some time.

2. In the light of the challenges of new product forecasting, it is usually a good idea to draw on a range of methods to produce forecasts, including statistical forecasting, market research, and management judgment. Where management judgment

is employed, it is best to structure the process to try to avoid psychological and motivational biases that may reduce forecast accuracy.

3. The process of structured analogies provides guidance to the forecaster so that available information and judgment can be used efficiently.

4. The Bass diffusion model is underpinned by a theory of how customers adopt new products. It can therefore provide an explanation for any observed patterns in uptake, and it can be particularly useful in forecasting products that are purchased once. However, the basic model is likely to be less effective when forecasting products where customers make multiple and repeated purchases and where marketing strategies such as price variations and promotions have a large influence on sales.

10.6 SUMMARY OF KEY TERMS

Advocacy bias. The tendency of judgmental forecasters to exaggerate the potential sales of a new product in anticipation that skeptical decision makers will discount their forecasts.

Forecasting by analogy. The process of using sales patterns of similar products that were launched in the past to produce sales forecasts for a new product.

Structured analogies. A structured process that is designed to support the identification of suitable groups of analogous products and the subsequent use of these to obtain sales forecasts for a new product.

Diffusion. The process through which a new product is taken up for the first time by customers in a given market over the periods following the product's launch.

Innovators. Consumers who buy a new product in response to advertising, promotions, or information in the mass media without knowledge of other consumers' experience of owning the product.

Imitators.	Consumers who buy a product, having heard about it from those who have already purchased it.
Bass diffusion model.	A model designed to represent the pattern of diffusion of a new product based on the behavior of innovators and imitators.
Coefficient of innovation (p).	A parameter in the Bass model that is designed to reflect the influence of advertising and the media on potential purchasers.
Coefficient of imitation (q).	A parameter in the Bass model that is designed to reflect the influence of word of mouth from existing customers on the propensity of potential customers to purchase a product.
Adopter.	A consumer who has made at least one purchase of a given product.

10.7 REFERENCES

Gilliland M., and Guseman, S. (2009–2010). Forecasting new products by structured analogy. *Journal of Business Forecasting*, 12–15.

Kahn, K. B (2006). *New Product Forecasting. An Applied Approach*. Armonk: M.E. Sharpe.

CHAPTER **11**

Summary: A Best Practice Blueprint for Using Your Software

11.1 INTRODUCTION

Demand forecasting is challenging and the performance of your forecasts depends largely on having the right facilities available in your software to support you in this task. In this last chapter, we will draw up a shopping list of desirable features of forecasting software products. We will then summarize the key messages in the book to provide a blueprint for best practice.

11.2 DESIRABLE CHARACTERISTICS OF FORECASTING SOFTWARE

In addition to obvious features – such as ease-of-use, speed, and accuracy of calculation, a wide range of available methods, the ability to interface with other systems, and the availability of training and support—there are a number of more specific characteristics to look for when choosing forecasting software. We discuss these here, and they are summarized in Table 11.1.

11.2.1 Data Preparation

Before you can start forecasting, you need to prepare your data. Ideally, forecasting software will have facilities for dealing with missing values and outliers. It should also enable you to make trading-day adjustments. Where a normal distribution cannot be assumed, the software should alert you to this and provide a facility for transforming the data to normality.

11.2.2 Graphical Displays

Clear graphical displays of your sales history are essential for you to apply sanity checks to any forecasts. They should allow you to spot unusual data points, seasonality, different types of trends, and intermittent demand. Seasonal-cycle graphs (like that shown in Figure 2.3) are also helpful in identifying seasonal patterns. Scattergraphs are essential when looking at possible relationships between sales and other

Table 11.1   Desirable Features of Forecasting Software

Desirable Feature	✓
Data Preparation	
Handles missing values	
Handles outliers	
Allows trading-day adjustments	
Allows transformations to meet model assumptions	
Graphical Displays	
Clear displays of sales history	
Seasonal-cycle graphs	
Scattergraphs	
Residual plots	
Method Selection	
Automatic method selection available	
Explanations for selection of methods	
Flagging of forecasts that need attention	
Separates fitting and out-of-sample periods	
Reports multiple measures of fit, accuracy, and bias	
Allows rolling-origin evaluation	
Implementing Methods	
Allows use of event indices	
Provides forecasts of predictor variables	
Supports forecasts from combinations of methods	
Supports temporal aggregation	
Hierarchies	
Supports top-down, bottom-up, and middle-out methods	
Copes with special events and intermittent demand	
Forecasting with Probabilities	
Provides probability distributions or prediction intervals	
Explains how prediction intervals (PIs) were estimated	
Provides flexibility in choice of coverage probabilities for PIs	
Indicates required safety stocks or reorder levels	

(*Continued*)

Table 11.1 *(Continued)*

Support for Judgment	
Allows judgmental interventions	
Allows judgmental interventions to be evaluated	
Provides databases of analogous cases	
Allows documentation of reasons for interventions	
Offers online advice and guidance on interventions	
Presentation of Forecasts	
Clear presentations of forecasts & how they relate to sales history	
Nontechnical explanations of rationale and assumptions of forecasts	
Clear indications of levels of uncertainty	

variables. Plots of residuals are useful when determining whether the forecasting method has extracted all the useful predictive information from the data or when checking its assumptions.

11.2.3 Method Selection

Facilities for the automatic selection of forecasting methods are highly desirable, especially if you have a large number of forecasts to make. However, the selection process should penalize more complex methods – using measures like the Bayesian information criterion (BIC), the Akaike information criterion (AIC), or adjusted R-squared. The process should be transparent with the system providing explanations for its selection. Good software will provide indications on whether a model's assumptions are valid. When the software generates hundreds of forecasts automatically on a regular basis, the ability to flag forecasts that need attention, due to large errors or biases, is crucial.

The software should provide a clear demarcation between fitting and out-of-sample periods when it reports on the performance of a method. It should also allow the user to determine the number of periods of each type. Multiple measures of fit and accuracy are also desirable – as we saw in Chapter 3, different accuracy measures have pros and cons, and none, on its own, is likely to provide a perfect measure of forecasting performance. Bias measures are important and, in some circumstances, can provide more useful information than accuracy metrics. In out-of-sample testing, there should be a facility for rolling-origin evaluation, so we can assess the performance of forecasts for different lead times.

11.2.4 Implementing Methods

When special or unusual events, like product promotions or extreme weather conditions, are likely to affect demand, software that allows you to create event indices is particularly useful, and it can obviate difficult decisions on whether to remove outliers from a sales history.

As we saw in Chapter 6, when applying regression analysis, one problem is that often we have to forecast the future values of the predictor variables themselves. When this is the case, a facility that provides extrapolations for these variables can be helpful.

Forecasting accuracy is often improved when software allows the user to combine the forecast of different methods. Improvements can also result when the software permits temporal aggregation of a sales history from high-frequency buckets, such as days to lower frequencies, such as weeks.

11.2.5 Hierarchies

Ideally, software should provide all three methods for reconciling forecasts in hierarchies – top-down, bottom-up, and middle-out. It should identify which approach is most appropriate and should be able to cope when products in the hierarchy are subject to special events or intermittent demand.

11.2.6 Forecasting with Probabilities

To support decisions on reorder levels and safety stocks, the software needs to go beyond point forecasts and provide forecasts that include estimates of the level of uncertainty associated with the forecasts. The ideal is to produce complete probability distributions of demand, but these are not usually available in current software – though this may be a future development. Most products produce prediction intervals instead. Because these tend to be too narrow, it is a good idea if we know how the software estimated them. For example, did it assume a normal distribution and did it take into account the added uncertainty of not knowing future values of predictor variables? In some cases, information on the method of estimation is not available, either in the software manual or within the online help function.

To help us to determine safety stocks, the software will need either to be flexible in the coverage probabilities it provides for prediction intervals, or it will need to indicate the safety stocks that are required directly. If it does neither of these things, then we will need to use the offline methods outlined in Chapter 7.

11.2.7   Support for Judgment

We have argued that judgmental overrides of software forecasts tend to be made too often. Nevertheless, forecasting software should have facilities that allow such interventions to be made when they are needed. While most products have this facility, they usually provide little or no guidance on whether an intervention is justified and, when it is, how large a change the forecaster should make to the software's forecast. Researchers have suggested a number of methods for enhancing the quality of judgmental interventions, but few if any have been implemented in commercial software products to date.

Ideally, we should be able to obtain metrics that tell us the extent to which judgmental interventions are improving, or reducing, the accuracy of forecasts. Other forms of support can include providing databases of analogous cases, allowing documentation of the reasons for interventions so the validity of these reasons can be assessed at a later date, and offering online advice and guidance that is dynamically adapted to each forecasting situation.

11.2.8   Presentation of Forecasts

Once we have the forecasts, we may need to convince other managers to trust them. Good quality software will allow for clear presentations of the forecasts, with graphs to show how they relate to sales histories.

Ideally, these presentations will include nontechnical explanations of the rationale and assumptions underlying the forecasts, together with indications of the level of uncertainty associated with them.

11.3   A BLUEPRINT FOR BEST PRACTICE

Forecasters often have a bad reputation. They are lambasted in the national press for failing to predict economic downturns or election results. In companies, other managers may perceive that sales forecasts are always wrong and not give them serious attention. Much of this disdain arises because people don't understand what a computer point forecast is. It's a prediction of the average outcome that would occur if the period we are forecasting was repeated many times over, with different sets of random events occurring each time. We can therefore say, for example, that if we spend $50,000 on advertising and charge a price of $4 per unit, on average we would expect to get sales of 34,500 units. We know that random events will, almost certainly, cause the actual sales to stray from this average. Computer forecasts therefore confine themselves to predicting systematic underlying patterns. Any attempt by the computer, or a person adjusting its forecast, to predict randomness will usually reduce the forecast's accuracy.

So what key messages for best practice does this imply?

First, restrict your judgmental interventions to circumstances where you have reliable information about a forthcoming event that is likely to have a big effect on sales – and that you know has not been factored into the computer forecasts. If you think an intervention is justified, document the reasons for making the change. Use forecast value added (FVA) analysis to assess whether judgmental interventions are improving accuracy.

Second, automating the forecasting process as far as possible can save time and reduce the effects of judgmental biases. This allows you to focus your efforts on investigating products where the software indicates that the forecasts are performing less well than expected.

Third, give your computer as much past data as possible to help it to separate the randomness in your sales history from underlying systematic patterns. If the underlying conditions have changed, either the computer will detect this or the forecasting method will usually adapt to the change (as long as it is not a global model).

Fourth, acknowledge that there is uncertainty surrounding a point forecast and make use of prediction intervals to represent this uncertainty and to estimate safety stock levels. However, bear in mind that prediction intervals generated by some software products tend to be too narrow and may need widening.

Fifth, judge the performance of a forecasting method by how well it predicts sales figures that it has not seen (i.e., sales in out-of-sample periods). Remember that measures of how well a method fits in-sample sales tend to overestimate the method's forecast accuracy.

Sixth, do not assume that more complex forecasting methods will necessarily produce more accurate forecasts. It is a good idea to compare a method's accuracy against that of a simpler benchmark method, such as a naïve forecast. Even if a complex method is more accurate, the extra accuracy may not be justified given the extra effort and costs it involves and its lack of transparency to other managers.

Seventh, don't forget to measure the bias in forecasts as well as their accuracy, but measure it over several periods so you are not tempted to overreact to a single freak figure.

Eighth, forecasting sales that have been aggregated, say from days to weeks, or weeks to months, is likely to lead to improved accuracy.

Ninth, combining the forecasts of different methods – usually by averaging them – can also lead to greater accuracy.

Tenth, remember that correlation does not prove causation.

Follow these guidelines and you will get the best out of your forecasting software – and that's a confident forecast.

11.4 REFERENCES

Goodwin, P. (2015). Where is the support for judgment? *Foresight: The International Journal of Applied Forecasting*, **39**, 14–15.

Goodwin, P (2017). *Forewarned: A Sceptic's Guide to Prediction*. London: Biteback Publications.

Tashman, L. J., and Hoover, D. G. (2001). Diffusion of forecasting principles through software. In: J.S. Armstrong (ed.). *Principles of Forecasting*. Boston: Kluwer Academic Publishers.

Index